MW01127579

THE SUPERNATURAL OCCURRENCES OF CHARLES G. FINNEY

Daniel R. Jennings

SEAN
MULTIMEDIA
www.seanmultimedia.com

The Supernatural Occurrences Of Charles G. Finney

Copyright © 2009 by Daniel R. Jennings

ISBN 978-1475237825

Jennings, Daniel, R. 1977-
The Supernatural Occurrences Of Charles G. Finney.

Scripture quotations, unless otherwise indicated, are from the King James Version, either modernized by the author or in their original form.

οτι ουκ αδυνατησει παρα του θεου παν ρημα

Lucas I.XXXVII

TABLE OF CONTENTS

Chapter 1

Charles G. Finney: A Biographical Sketch

Charles G. Finney

Charles Grandison Finney (1792-1875) was a lawyer who, after converting to Christianity, became one of the foremost American ministers of his day. His ministry efforts played a central part in a widespread 19th century revival of American Christianity and his theological emphases and innovations in church practice influenced not only his own time but have continued to influence American Christianity up until the 21st century. Theologically these facets include the belief that Jesus died for all men, that infants who die will go to Heaven, that mankind is endowed with free will and that all men are capable of either choosing or rejecting Christ immediately at any time. On the practical side innovations such as protracted "revival" meetings, altar calls, the use of music during appeals to persons encouraging them to make decisions for Christ and the use of sermon outlines as opposed to writing out and reading the entire sermon also owe their acceptance in modern day American Christianity to Finney. To conservatives Finney stands as an evangelical giant who was one of the leaders in a revival during which 50,000 persons a week were getting saved. To liberals Finney is regarded as a forerunner of the modern social gospel movement because of his tireless efforts in working to end American slavery. His writings had a profound influence on a young William Booth who would go on to found the Salvation Army and D. L. Moody encouraged the world to "Look at the praying Finney, whose prayers, faith, sermons and writings, have shaken this whole country".[1] Charles Spurgeon, though disagreeing with him theologically, thought highly enough of Finney to quote him as an authority on evangelism[2] and when an artist named Jack Chick was given a book of his articles entitled *Power From On High* he was inspired to create the Chick Tracts witnessing booklets. Nearly 70 years after his death V. Raymond Edman, president of Wheaton College, referred to Finney as "the most widely known and most successful American evangelist."[3] His book *Finney Lives On* carried with it an endorsement by Billy Graham. In 1960 Harvard University Press, demonstrating the impact that Finney's revival measures had had upon American culture, released a critical edition of his *Revival Lectures*. Jerry Falwell referred to him as *"one of my greatest heroes"*[4] and today, some 135 years after his death the majority of his books are still in print.[5]

---

[1] Moody, D. L. *Prevailing Prayer: What Hinders It?* (Chicago: F. H. Revell, 1884), Ch. 1, p.14-15

[2] Spurgeon, Charles. *The Soul-Winner, or How To Lead Sinners To The Saviour* (London: Passmore & Alabaster, 1903), Ch. 4: Sermons Likely To Win Souls

[3] Edman, V. Raymond. *Finney Lives On: The Man, His Revival Methods, And His Message* (New York: Fleming H. Revell, 1951), p.15

[4] Jerry Falwell, interview in *The Horse's Mouth* (September, 1994) published by Christians United for Reformation (CURE), in Anaheim, California.

[5] Through companies such as Zondervan and Whitaker but most notably through Truth In Heart Publishing who are also working on completion of

In evaluating an individual of this stature certain questions come to the forefront. Finney's impact upon the church of Christ is undeniable and similar in nature to the revival of interest in Christianity that occurred in the book of Acts: Were there any similarities between the way that God called New Testament persons such as the Apostle Paul and Finney? Were the responses of the people to Finney's messages comparable in any way to the response of the people to the preaching of the first Christian ministers? Were the unusual experiences mentioned frequently in the book of Acts similar in any respect to the unusual experiences mentioned frequently by Finney? Does God deal with Christian leaders today in the same way that He dealt with the first century Christian leaders? And finally, could studying Finney's life help to give us a more understandable picture of what those who ministered in the first century experienced on an emotional, physical and spiritual level?

The quotes used in this investigation, unless otherwise indicated, are from Finney's *Memoirs*[6] and are included to show similarities between his experiences and those of Christians living in the first century church.

---

the 20 volume *The Life and Works of Charles G. Finney* which is scheduled to include items never before published.

[6] First published by Fleming H. Revell Company in 1876 under the title *Memoirs Of Rev. Charles G. Finney* it has also appeared with the titles *An Autobiography* (Salvation Army Book Department, 1880) and *Charles G. Finney: An Autobiography* (Hodder and Stoughton, 1882).

Chapter 2

Revelations From The Holy Spirit

Throughout his *Memoirs* Finney mentions having experienced revelations from the Lord. These revelations were the supernatural revealing of a certain truth to Finney, in some cases regarding his own spiritual condition. Both Jesus and Paul speak of God the Father revealing things to men supernaturally.[7] After studying the life of Finney one is led to ask, in what way(s) did his revelations compare or differ from the revelations of the Spirit mentioned by both Jesus and Paul.

A Supernatural Revelation
Leads To Finney's Salvation

Tuesday night I had become very nervous; and in the night a strange feeling came over me as if I was about to die. I knew that if I did I should sink down to hell; but I quieted myself as best I could until morning. At an early hour I started for the office. But just before I arrived at the office, something seemed to confront me with questions like these: indeed, it seemed as if the inquiry was within myself, as if an inward voice said to me, "What are you waiting for? Did you not promise to give your heart to God? And what are you trying to do? Are you endeavoring to work out a righteousness of your own?"

Just at this point the whole question of Gospel salvation opened to my mind in a manner most marvelous to me at the time. <u>I think I then saw, as clearly as I ever have in my life, the reality and fullness of the atonement</u>

---

[7] Matthew 16:17; Galatians 1:11-12; 2Corinthians 12:1

of Christ. I saw that his work was a finished work; and that instead of having, or needing, any righteousness of my own to recommend me to God, I had to submit myself to the righteousness of God through Christ. Gospel salvation seemed to me to be an offer of something to be accepted; and that it was full and complete; and that all that was necessary on my part, was to get my own consent to give up my sins, and accept Christ.[8] Salvation, it seemed to me, instead of being a thing to be wrought out, by my own works, was a thing to be found entirely in the Lord Jesus Christ, who presented himself before me as my God and my Savior.[9]

Without being distinctly aware of it, I had stopped in the street right where the inward voice seemed to arrest me. How long I remained in that position I cannot say. But after this distinct revelation had stood for some little time before my mind, the question seemed to be put, "Will you accept it now, today?" I replied, "Yes; I will accept it today, or I will die in the attempt."

North of the village, and over a hill, lay a piece of woods, in which I was in the almost daily habit of walking, more or less, when it was pleasant weather...instead of

---

[8] This revelation is interesting because it went against the grain of what Finney had been taught as a Presbyterian. As a Presbyterian he had been taught to believe in predestination and that no person could choose of their "own consent" to give up their sins and "accept" Christ. They had to wait and see if he chose them as one of the predestined who were elect to salvation. This radical new way of understanding salvation, which differed greatly from the indoctrination that Finney had received, gives credence to this being a genuine revelation from the Spirit.

[9] Jesus talks about God the Father revealing supernaturally to Simon Peter that Jesus was "the Christ, the Son of the living God" (Mat 16:17). Paul testifies that the gospel which he preached was "received...by the revelation of Jesus Christ" (Gal 1:11-12). In what ways, if any, did Finney's revelation of salvation through Jesus Christ differ from Peter and Paul's?

going to the office, I turned and bent my course toward the woods, feeling that I must be alone, and away from all human eyes and ears, so that I could pour out my prayer to God. But still my pride must show itself. As I went over the hill, it occurred to me that someone might see me and suppose that I was going away to pray. Yet probably there was not a person on earth that would have suspected such a thing, had he seen me going. But so great was my pride, and so much was I possessed with the fear of man, that I recollect that I skulked along under the fence, till I got so far out of sight that no one from the village could see me. I then penetrated into the woods, I should think, a quarter of a mile, went over on the other side of the hill, and found a place where some large trees had fallen across each other, leaving an open place between. There I saw I could make a kind of closet. I crept into this place and knelt down for prayer. As I turned to go up into the woods, I recollect to have said, "I will give my heart to God, or I never will come down from there."...

But when I attempted to pray I found that my heart would not pray. I had supposed that if I could only be where I could speak aloud, without being overheard, I could pray freely. But lo! when I came to try, I was dumb; that is, I had nothing to say to God; or at least I could say but a few words, and those without heart. In attempting to pray I would hear a rustling in the leaves, as I thought, and would stop and look up to see if somebody were not coming. This I did several times.

Finally I found myself verging fast to despair. I said to myself, "I cannot pray. My heart is dead to God, and will not pray." I then reproached myself for having promised to give my heart to God before I left the woods. When I came to try, I found I could not give my heart to

6

God. My inward soul hung back, and there was no going out of my heart to God. I began to feel deeply that it was too late; that it must be that I was given up of God and was past hope.

The thought was pressing me of the rashness of my promise, that I would give my heart to God that day or die in the attempt. It seemed to me as if that was binding upon my soul; and yet I was going to break my vow. A great sinking and discouragement came over me, and I felt almost too weak to stand upon my knees.

Just at this moment I again thought I heard someone approach me, and I opened my eyes to see whether it were so. <u>But right there the revelation of my pride of heart, as the great difficulty that stood in the way, was distinctly shown to me. An overwhelming sense of my wickedness in being ashamed to have a human being see me on my knees before God, took such powerful possession of me, that I cried at the top of my voice, and exclaimed that I would not leave that place if all the men on earth and all the devils in hell surrounded me.</u>[10] "What!" I said, "such a degraded sinner I am, on my knees confessing my sins to the great and holy God; and ashamed to have any human being, and a sinner like myself, find me on my knees endeavoring to make my peace with my offended God!" The sin appeared awful, infinite. It broke me down before the Lord.

Just at that point this passage of Scripture seemed to drop into my mind with a flood of light: "Then shall ye go and pray unto me, and I will hearken unto you. Then

---

[10] Paul talks about men who "speak…by revelation" (1Co 14:6), and says of himself "I will come to…revelations of the Lord" (2Co 12:1) and that it was "by revelation" that God had given him knowledge concerning "the mystery of Christ" (Eph 3:3-4). In what ways, if any, do these revelations differ from the ones experienced by Finney?

shall ye seek me and find me, when ye shall search for me with all your heart."[11] I instantly seized hold of this with my heart. I had intellectually believed the Bible before; but never had the truth been in my mind that faith was a voluntary trust instead of an intellectual state. I was as conscious as I was of my existence, of trusting at that moment in God's veracity. <u>Somehow I knew that that was a passage of Scripture, though I do not think I had ever read it. I knew that it was God's word, and God's voice, as it were, that spoke to me.</u>[12] I cried to Him, "Lord, I take thee at thy word. Now thou knowest that I do search for thee with all my heart, and that I have come here to pray to thee; and thou hast promised to hear me."

That seemed to settle the question that I could then, that day, perform my vow. The Spirit seemed to lay stress upon that idea in the text, "When you search for me with all your heart." The question of when, that is of the present time, seemed to fall heavily into my heart. I told the Lord that I should take him at his word; that he could not lie;[13] and that therefore I was sure that he heard my prayer, and that he would be found of me. <u>He then gave me many other promises, both from the Old and the New Testament, especially some most precious promises respecting our Lord Jesus Christ. I never can, in words, make any human being understand how precious and true those promises appeared to me. I took them one after the other as infallible truth, the assertions of God who could not lie. They did not seem so much to fall into my intellect as into my heart, to be put within the grasp of the voluntary powers of my mind; and I seized hold of</u>

---

[11] Jeremiah 29:12-13

[12] Is this an example of the "word of knowledge" mentioned in 1Corinthians 12:8?

[13] Titus 1:2

them, appropriated them, and fastened upon them with the grasp of a drowning man.[14]

I continued thus to pray, and to receive and appropriate promises for a long time, I know not how long. I prayed till my mind became so full that, before I was aware of it, I was on my feet and tripping up the ascent toward the road. The question of my being converted, had not so much as arisen to my thought; but as I went up, brushing through the leaves and bushes, I recollect saying with emphasis, "If I am ever converted, I will preach the Gospel."[15]

The Holy Spirit Reveals A Coming Revival

I should have said that, while I was at Brownville, God revealed to me, all at once, in a most unexpected manner, the fact that he was going to pour out his Spirit at Gouverneur, and that I must go there and preach. Of the place I knew absolutely nothing, except that, in that town there was so much opposition manifested to the revival in Antwerp, the year before. I can never tell how, or why, the Spirit of God made that revelation to me. But I knew then, and I have no doubt now, that it was a direct revelation from God to me. I had not thought of the place, that I know of, for months; but in prayer the thing was all shown to me, as clear as light, that I must go and preach in Gouverneur, and that God would pour out his Spirit there.

Very soon after this, I saw one of the members of the church from Gouverneur, who was passing through Brownville. I told him what God had revealed to me. He stared at me as if he supposed that I was insane. But I

---

[14] In what sense could this be compared to the concept of "revelation" as it is found in Matthew 16:17, 1Corinthians 14:26, 2Corinthians 12:1, and Galatians 1:12?

[15] Ch. 2

charged him to go home, and tell the brethren what I said, that they might prepare themselves for my coming, and for the outpouring of the Lord's Spirit. From him I learned that they had no minister; that there were two churches and two meeting houses, in the town, standing near together; that the Baptists had a minister, and the Presbyterians no minister; that an elderly minister lived there who had formerly been their pastor, but had been dismissed; and that they were having, in the Presbyterian church, no regular Sabbath services. From what he said, I gathered that religion was in a very low state; and he himself was as cold as an iceberg…I preached a few times at this place[16], and then the question of Gouverneur came up again; and God seemed to say to me, "Go to Gouverneur; the time has come."[17] Brother Nash[18] had come a few days before this, and was spending some time with me. At the time of this last call to Gouverneur, I had some two or three appointments ahead, in that part of Rutland. I said therefore to brother Nash, "You must go to Gouverneur and see what is there, and come back and make your report."

He started the next morning, and after he had been gone two or three days, returned, saying, that he had found a good many professors of religion, under considerable exercise of mind, and that he was confident that there was a good deal of the Spirit of the Lord among the people; but that they were not aware what the state of

---

[16] Brownville.

[17] In Acts 10:19-20 the Holy Spirit spoke to Peter telling him to go to with three men (who took him to Caesarea) and in Acts 16:6-9 Paul and his companions were kept by the Holy Spirit from preaching in Asia. How did the Holy Spirit's leading of Peter and Paul differ from the Holy Spirit's leading of Finney?

[18] That is, Rev. Daniel Nash (1775-1831) an older minister who served as Finney's prayer partner.

things really was. I then informed the people where I was preaching, that I was called to Gouverneur, and could make no more appointments to preach in that place. I requested Brother Nash to return immediately, informing the people that they might expect me on a certain day that week...I do not know the number of those converted in that revival [in Gouverneur]. It was a large farming town, settled by well-to-do inhabitants. The great majority of them, I am confident, were, in that revival, converted to Christ.[19]

A Revelation Of The Spirit Teaches
Finney How To Lead A Man To Christ

The father of Judge C— who was at Albany with me, was living with his son whose guest I was at the time. The old gentleman had been a judge in Vermont. He was remarkably correct in his outward life, a venerable man, whose house, in Vermont, had been the home of ministers who visited the place; and he was to all appearance quite satisfied with his amiable and self-righteous life. His wife had told me of her anxiety for his conversion, and his son had repeatedly expressed fear that his father's self-righteousness would never be overcome, and that his natural amiability would ruin his soul.

One Sabbath morning, the Holy Spirit opened the case to my apprehension, and showed me how to reach it. In a few moments I had the whole subject in my mind. I went down stairs, and told the old lady and her son what I was about to do, and exhorted them to pray earnestly for him. I followed out the divine showing, and the word took such powerful hold of him that he spent a sleepless night. His wife informed me that he had spent a night of

---

[19] Ch. 9, 10

11

anguish, that his self-righteousness was thoroughly annihilated, and that he was almost in despair. His son had told me that he had long prided himself, as being better than members of the church. He soon became clearly converted, and lived a Christian life to the end.[20]

A Revelation Of What Life In Heaven Is Like

A few years after this season of refreshing, that beloved wife, of whom I have spoken, died. This was to me a great affliction. However, I did not feel any murmuring, or the least resistance to the will of God. I gave her up to God, without any resistance whatever, that I can recollect. But it was to me a great sorrow. The night after she died, I was lying in my room alone, and some Christian friends were sitting up in the parlor, and watching out the night. I had been asleep for a little while, and as I awoke, the thought of my bereavement flashed over my mind with such power! My wife was gone! I should never hear her speak again, nor see her face! Her children were motherless! What should I do? My brain seemed to reel, as if my mind would swing from its pivot. I rose instantly from my bed, exclaiming, "I shall be deranged if I cannot rest in God" The Lord soon calmed my mind, for that night; but still, at times, seasons of sorrow would come over me, that were almost overwhelming.

One day I was upon my knees, communing with God upon the subject, and all at once he seemed to say to me, "You loved your wife?"

"Yes," I said.

"Well, did you love her for her own sake, or for your sake? Did you love her, or yourself? If you loved her for her own sake, why do you sorrow that she is with me?

---

[20] *Ch. 16*

12

Should not her happiness with me, make you rejoice instead of mourn, if you loved her for her own sake?"

"Did you love her," he seemed to say to me, "for my sake? If you loved her for my sake, surely you would not grieve that she is with me. Why do you think of your loss, and lay so much stress upon that, instead of thinking of her gain? Can you be sorrowful, when she is so joyful and happy? If you loved her for her own sake, would you not rejoice in her joy, and be happy in her happiness?"

I can never describe the feelings that came over me, when I seemed to be thus addressed. It produced an instantaneous change in the whole state of my mind. From that moment, sorrow, on account of my loss, was gone forever. I no longer thought of my wife as dead, but as alive, and in the midst of the glories of heaven. My faith was, at this time, so strong and my mind so enlightened, that it seemed as if I could enter into the very state of mind in which she was, in heaven; and if there is any such thing as communing with an absent spirit, or with one who is in heaven, I seemed to commune with her. Not that I ever supposed she was present in such a sense that I communed personally with her. But it seemed as if I knew what her state of mind was there, what profound, unbroken rest, in the perfect will of God. I could see that was heaven; and I experienced it in my own soul. I have never to this day, lost the blessing of these views. They frequently recur to me, as the very state of mind in which the inhabitants of heaven are, and I can see why they are in such a state of blessedness.[21]

---

[21] *Ch. 27*

Chapter 3

Visions

Three times during the course of his life Finney recorded having a vision. Several persons from the New Testament to include the women at the tomb,[22] Ananias,[23] Cornelius,[24] Peter,[25] Paul,[26] and John,[27] all experienced visions. Ananias, Paul and John each experienced a vision of Jesus himself. After studying the life of Finney, one is led to ask in what way(s) did his visions compare or differ from the visions experienced by these first century Christians?

A Vision Of Jesus

Just before evening the thought took possession of my mind, that as soon as I was left alone in the new office, I would try to pray again — that I was not going to abandon the subject of religion and give it up, at any rate; and therefore, although I no longer had any concern about my soul, still I would continue to pray.[28]

By evening we got the books and furniture adjusted; and I made up, in an open fireplace, a good fire, hoping to spend the evening alone. Just at dark Squire W—[29], seeing that everything was adjusted, bade me goodnight

---

[22] Luke 24:22-23

[23] Acts 9:10-16

[24] Acts 10:1-8

[25] Acts 10:9-19

[26] Acts 16:6-10, 18:9-11, 26:12-23

[27] Revelation 9:17

[28] This event happened in connection with Finney's conversion.

[29] That is, Benjamin Wright (1784-1861), a lawyer with whom Finney worked.

and went to his home. I had accompanied him to the door; and as I closed the door and turned around, my heart seemed to be liquid within me. All my feelings seemed to rise and flow out; and the utterance of my heart was, "I want to pour my whole soul out to God." The rising of my soul was so great that I rushed into the room back of the front office, to pray.

There was no fire, and no light, in the room; nevertheless it appeared to me as if it were perfectly light.[30] As I went in and shut the door after me, it seemed as if <u>I met the Lord Jesus Christ face to face</u>. It did not occur to me then, nor did it for some time afterward, that <u>it was wholly a mental state</u>.[31] On the contrary it seemed to me that <u>I saw him as I would see any other man</u>. He said nothing, but looked at me in such a manner as to break me right down at his feet. I have always since regarded this as <u>a most remarkable state of mind; for it seemed to me a reality</u>, that he stood before me, and I fell down at his feet and poured out my soul to him. I wept aloud like a child, and made such confessions as I could with my choked utterance. It seemed to me that I bathed his feet with my tears; and yet I had no distinct impression that I touched him, that I recollect.

I must have continued in this state for a good while; but my mind was too much absorbed with the interview to recollect anything that I said. But I know, as soon as my mind became calm enough to break off from the interview, I returned to the front office, and found that the fire that I had made of large wood was nearly burned out.[32]

---

[30] Compare Acts 22:6, 9.

[31] This indicates that this experience was a vision.

[32] *Ch. 2.* The Apostle Paul was converted through a vision of Jesus Christ accompanied by a bright light (Ac 9:1-8). A vision of Jesus Christ in a

15

A Vision Of The Light Of God's Glory

I had been in the habit of rising early in the morning, and spending a season of prayer alone in the meeting house; and I finally succeeded in interesting a considerable number of brethren to meet me there in the morning for a prayer meeting. This was at a very early hour; and we were generally together long before it was light enough to see to read. I persuaded my minister to attend these morning meetings. But soon they began to be remiss; whereupon I would get up in time to go around to their houses and wake them up. Many times I went round and round, and called the brethren that I thought would be most likely to attend, and we would have a precious season of prayer. But still the brethren, I found, attended with more and more reluctance; which fact greatly tried me.

One morning I had been around and called the brethren up, and when I returned to the meeting house but few of them had got there. Mr. Gale, my minister, was standing at the door of the church, and as I came up, all at once the glory of God shone upon and round about me, in a manner most marvelous.[33] The day was just beginning to dawn. But all at once a light perfectly ineffable shone in my soul, that almost prostrated me to the ground. In this light it seemed as if I could see that all nature praised and worshipped God except man. This light seemed to be like the brightness of the sun in every direction. It was too intense for the eyes. I recollect casting my eyes down and breaking into a flood of tears,

---

room that became supernaturally lit also played an instrumental part in the conversion of Finney. In what way(s), if any, did Finney's vision differ from Paul's?

[33] Compare Luke 2:8-9.

16

in view of the fact that mankind did not praise God. I think I knew something then, by actual experience, of that light that prostrated Paul on his way to Damascus.[34] It was surely a light such as I could not have endured long. When I burst out into such loud weeping, Mr. Gale said, "What is the matter, brother Finney?" I could not tell him. I found that he had seen no light; and that he saw no reason why I should be in such a state of mind. I therefore said but little. I believe I merely replied, that I saw the glory of God; and that I could not endure to think of the manner in which he was treated by men. Indeed, it did not seem to me at the time that the vision of his glory which I had, was to be described in words. I wept it out; and the vision, if it may be so called, passed away and left my mind calm.[35]

A Vision Encourages Finney To Keep On Ministering

However, until I arrived at Auburn, I was not fully aware of the amount of opposition I was destined to meet, from the ministry; not the ministry in the region where I had labored; but from ministers where I had not labored, and who knew personally nothing of me, but were influenced by the false reports which they heard. But soon after I arrived at Auburn, I learned from various sources that a system of espionage was being carried on, that was destined to result, and intended to result, in an extensive union of ministers and churches to hedge me in, and prevent the spread of the revivals in connection with my labors...I shall never forget what a scene I passed through one day in my room at Dr. Lansing's. The Lord showed me as in a vision what was before me. He

---

[34] Acts 9:3-4

[35] *Ch. 3.* In what way(s), if any, did this vision differ from the vision had by Ananias in Acts 9:10-16?

drew so near to me, while I was engaged in prayer, that my flesh literally trembled on my bones. I shook from head to foot, under a full sense of the presence of God. At first, and for some time, it seemed more like being on the top of Sinai, amidst its full thundering, than in the presence of the cross of Christ.[36]

Never in my life, that I recollect, was I so awed and humbled before God as then. Nevertheless, instead of feeling like fleeing, I seemed drawn nearer and nearer to God — seemed to draw nearer and nearer to that Presence that filled me with such unutterable awe and trembling. After a season of great humiliation before him, there came a great lifting up. God assured me that he would be with me and uphold me; that no opposition should prevail against me; that I had nothing to do, in regard to all this matter, but to keep about my work, and wait for the salvation of God. The sense of God's presence, and all that passed between God and my soul at that time, I can never describe. It led me to be perfectly trustful, perfectly calm, and to have nothing but the most perfectly kind feelings toward all the brethren that were misled, and were arraying themselves against me. I felt assured that all would come out right; that my true course was to leave everything to God, and to keep about my work; and as the storm gathered and the opposition increased, I never for one moment doubted how it would result. I was never disturbed by it, I never spent a waking hour in thinking of it; when to all outward appearance, it seemed as if all the churches of the land, except where I had labored, would unite to shut me out of their pulpits. This was indeed the avowed determination, as I understood, of the men that led in the opposition. They were so deceived that they thought there was no effectual

---

[36] Exodus 19:16, 20:18

way but to unite, and, as they expressed it, "put him down." But God assured me that they could not put me down.[37]

---

[37] *Ch. 15.* When Paul was in Corinth the Lord appeared to him in a vision telling him "Do not be afraid, but speak and do not hold your peace: For I am with you and no man shall set on you to hurt you... (Ac 18:9-10)." In what way(s), if any, did Finney's vision in which God told him that He was with him and that everything would be okay and that he should just keep going about his ministry differ from Paul's? In Acts 11:5 Peter describes a vision that he experienced while praying. In what way(s), if any, did Finney's experience of having a vision while praying differ from Peter's?

Chapter 4

The Gift Of Prophecy

Joel's prophecy of the coming of the Holy Spirit, which began to be fulfilled at Pentecost, indicated that the ministry of the Holy Spirit would include endowing men and women with the gift of prophecy.[38] This is seen, for example, in the ministry of Agabus[39], in the prophets of Antioch[40], Judas and Silas[41], the Ephesian converts[42], Philip's four daughters[43], Timothy[44], men and women in the Corinthian Church[45] and John[46]. Finney recorded several instances that appeared to be occurrences of the gift of prophecy. After reading them one is left to ask in what way(s), if any, did Finney's experiences with the gift of prophecy differ from those described in the New Testament?

Brother Nash's Prophecy

I have said that there was a Baptist church, and a Presbyterian, each having a meeting house standing upon the green, not far apart; and that the Baptist church had a pastor, but the Presbyterian had none. As soon as the revival broke out, and attracted general attention, the

---

[38] Joel 2:28-32
[39] Acts 11:27-28, 21:10-14
[40] Acts 13:1
[41] Acts 15:32
[42] Acts 19:1-6
[43] Acts 21:8-9
[44] 1Timothy 1:18-20, 4:14-15
[45] 1Corinthians 11:1-7
[46] Revelation 1:3, 10:11

Baptist brethren began to oppose it. They spoke against it, and used very objectionable means indeed to arrest its progress. This encouraged a set of young men to join hand in hand, to strengthen each other in opposition to the work. The Baptist church was quite influential; and the stand that they took greatly emboldened the opposition, and seemed to give it a peculiar bitterness and strength, as might be expected. Those young men seemed to stand like a bulwark in the way of the progress of the work.

In this state of things, brother Nash[47] and myself, after consultation, made up our minds that that thing must be overcome by prayer, and that it could not be reached in any other way. We therefore retired to a grove and gave ourselves up to prayer until we prevailed, and we felt confident that no power which earth or hell could interpose, would be allowed permanently to stop the revival.

The next Sabbath, after preaching morning and afternoon myself — for I did the preaching altogether, and brother Nash gave himself up almost continually to prayer — we met at five o'clock in the church, for a prayer meeting. The meeting house was filled. Near the close of the meeting, brother Nash arose, and addressed that company of young men who had joined hand in hand to resist the revival. I believe they were all there, and they sat braced up against the Spirit of God. It was too solemn for them really to make ridicule of what they heard and saw; and yet their brazen-facedness and stiff-neckedness were apparent to everybody. Brother Nash addressed them very earnestly, and pointed out the guilt and danger of the course they were taking. Toward the close of his address, he waxed exceeding warm, and said to them,

---

[47] That is, the aforementioned Rev. Daniel Nash.

"Now, mark me, young men! God will break your ranks in less than one week, either by converting some of you, or by sending some of you to hell. He will do this as certainly as the Lord is my God!" He was standing where he brought his hand down on the top of the pew before him, so as to make it thoroughly jar. He sat immediately down, dropped his head, and groaned with pain. The house was as still as death, and most of the people held down their heads. I could see that the young men were agitated. For myself, I regretted that brother Nash had gone so far. He had committed himself, that God would either take the life of some of them, and send them to hell, or convert some of them, within a week. However on Tuesday morning of the same week, the leader of these young men came to me, in the greatest distress of mind. He was all prepared to submit; and as soon as I came to press him he broke down like a child, confessed, and manifestly gave himself to Christ. Then he said, "What shall I do, Mr. Finney?" I replied "Go immediately to all your young companions, and pray with them, and exhort them, at once to turn to the Lord." He did so; and before the week was out, nearly if not all of that class of young men, were hoping in Christ.[48]

A Prophecy Foretells A
Woman's Healing And Conversion

The Lord taught me, in those early days of my Christian experience, many very important truths in regard to the spirit of prayer. Not long after I was converted, a woman with whom I had boarded — though I did not board with her at this time, was taken very sick.

---

[48] *Ch. 10.* Was this merely a coincidence, the power of persuasion or a real experience of God revealing what lay ahead for these impenitent sinners to a man who "gave himself up almost continually to prayer"?

She was not a Christian, but her husband was a professor of religion. He came into our office one evening, being a brother of Squire W—, and said to me, "My wife cannot live through the night." This seemed to plant an arrow, as it were, in my heart. It came upon me in the sense of a burden that crushed me, the nature of which I could not at all understand; but with it came an intense desire to pray for that woman. The burden was so great that I left the office almost immediately, and went up to the meeting house, to pray for her. There I struggled, but could not say much. I could only groan with groanings loud and deep.[49]

I stayed a considerable time in the church, in this state of mind, but got no relief. I returned to the office; but could not sit still. I could only walk the room and agonize. I returned to the meeting house again, and went through the same process of struggling. For a long time I tried to get my prayer before the Lord; but somehow words could not express it. I could only groan and weep, without being able to express what I wanted in words. I returned to the office again, and still found I was unable to rest; and I returned a third time to the meeting house. At this time the Lord gave me power to prevail. I was enabled to roll the burden upon him; and I obtained the assurance in my own mind that the woman would not die, and indeed that she would never die in her sins.

I returned to the office. My mind was perfectly quiet; and I soon left and retired to rest. Early the next morning the husband of this woman came into the office. I inquired how his wife was. He, smiling said, "She's alive, and to all appearance better this morning." I replied, "Brother W—, she will not die with this sickness; you may rely upon it. And she will never die in her sins." I do not know how I

---

[49] Compare Romans 8:23, 26.

was made sure of this; but it was in some way made plain to me, so that I had no doubt that she would recover. She did recover, and soon after obtained a hope in Christ.[50]

The Gift Of Prophecy Leads To Conviction

I recollect that one Sabbath morning, while I was preaching, I was describing the manner in which some men would oppose their families, and if possible, prevent their being converted. I gave so vivid a description of a case of this kind, that I said, "Probably if I were acquainted with you, I could call some of you by name, who treat your families in this manner." At this instant a man cried out in the congregation, "Name me!" and then threw his head forward on the seat before him; and it was plain that he trembled with great emotion. It turned out that he was treating his family in this manner; and that morning had done the same things that I had named. He said, his crying out, "Name me!" was so spontaneous and irresistible that he could not help it. But I fear he was never converted to Christ.[51]

---

[50] *Ch. 3.* Paul mentions things being revealed to people prophetically in 1Corinthians 14:30. In what way(s), if any, did God revealing to Finney that this woman would recover and turn to Christ before it happened differ from the experience that Paul was talking about?

[51] *Ch. 15.* One way that Paul describes the gift of prophecy is by stating that sometimes God will prophetically reveal the sins of a person attending the church to the speaker who will reveal them publicly. When the attendee hears this they will be struck in their conscience and acknowledge that God is in the church (1Co 14:24-25). Charles Spurgeon (1834-1892) mentioned having this happen to him more than a dozen times stating:

"Some months ago, whilst standing here preaching, I deliberately pointed to a man in the midst of the crowd, and said these words- 'There is a man sitting there that is a shoemaker, keeps his shop open on Sunday, had his shop open last Sabbath morning, took ninepence, and there was fourpence profit out of it. His soul is sold to Satan for

24

Finney Appears To Prophetically
Foretell An Animal's Strange Behavior

Soon after the adjournment of the convention, on the Sabbath, as I came out of the pulpit, a young lady by the name of S—, from Stephentown, was introduced to me. She asked me if I could not go up to their town and preach. I replied, that my hands were full, and that I did not see that I could...On the next Sabbath, Miss S— met me again, as I came out of the pulpit, and begged me to go up there and preach...Accordingly the next Sabbath,

---

fourpence.' A City Missionary, when going round the West end of the town met with a poor man, of whom he asked this question: 'Do you know Mr. Spurgeon?'...'Yes,' he said, 'I have every reason to know him; I have been to hear him, and under God's grace I have become a new man. But,' said he, 'shall I tell you how it was? I went to the Music Hall, and took my seat in the middle of the place, and the man looked at me as if he knew me, and deliberately told the congregation that I was a shoemaker, and that I sold shoes on Sunday; and I did, sir. But, sir, I should not have minded that; but he said I took ninepence the Sunday before, and that there was fourpence profit; and so I did take ninepence, and fourpence was just the profit, and how he should know that I'm sure I can not tell. It struck me it was God had spoken to my soul through him; and I shut my shop last Sunday, and was afraid to open it and go there, lest he should split about me again.'

I could tell as many as a dozen authentic stories of cases that have happened in this Hall, where I have deliberately pointed at somebody, without the slightest knowledge of the person, or ever having in the least degree any inkling or idea that what I said was right, except that I believed I was moved thereto by the Spirit; and so striking has been the description, that the persons have gone away and said, 'Come, see a man that told me all things that ever I did: he was sent of God to my soul, beyond a doubt, or else he could not have painted my case so clearly.'" (*Sermons Of The Rev. C.H. Spurgeon, Of London, Fourth Series, Sermon 10: God-The All-Seeing One* [New York: Sheldon, Blakeman & Co., 1858])

In what way(s), if any, did Finney and Spurgeon's experience differ from the prophetical experience that Paul described in 1Corinthians 14:24-25?

after preaching the second time, one of the young converts at New Lebanon offered to take me up to Stephentown in his carriage. When he came in his buggy to take me, I asked him, "Have you a steady horse?"

"O yes!" he replied, "perfectly so;" and smiling, asked, "What made you ask the question?"

"Because," I replied, "if the Lord wants me to go to Stephentown, the devil will prevent it if he can; and if you have not a steady horse, he will try to make him kill me." He smiled, and we rode on; and, strange to tell, before we got there, that horse ran away twice, and came near killing us. His owner expressed the greatest astonishment, and said he had never known such a thing before.[52]

A Woman Prophesies The Coming Revival

In the meantime, my own mind was much exercised in prayer; and I found that the spirit of prayer was prevailing, especially among the female members of the church. Mrs. B — and Mrs. H—, the wives of two of the elders of the church, I found, were, almost immediately, greatly exercised in prayer. Each of them had families of unconverted children; and they laid hold in prayer with an earnestness that, to me, gave promise that their families must be converted. Mrs. H—, however, was a woman of very feeble health, and had not ventured out much, to any meeting, for a long time. But, as the day was pleasant, she was out at the prayer meeting to which I have alluded, and seemed to catch the inspiration of that meeting, and took it home with her.

It was the next week, I think, that I called in at Mr. H—'s, and found him pale and agitated. He said to me "Brother Finney, I think my wife will die. She is so

---

[52] *Ch. 17*

26

exercised in her mind that she cannot rest day or night, but is given up entirely to prayer. She has been all the morning," said he, "in her room, groaning and struggling in prayer; and I am afraid it will entirely overcome her strength." Hearing my voice in the sitting room, she came out from her bedroom, and upon her face was a most heavenly glow. Her countenance was lighted up with a hope and a joy that were plainly from heaven. She exclaimed, "Brother Finney, the Lord has come! This work will spread over all this region! A cloud of mercy overhangs us all; and we shall see such a work of grace as we have never yet seen." Her husband looked surprised, confounded, and knew not what to say. It was new to him, but not to me. I had witnessed such scenes before, and believed that prayer had prevailed; nay, I felt sure of it in my own soul.[53]

A Prophecy Of A Coming
Revival To Rochester, New York

I have not said much, as yet, of the spirit of prayer that prevailed in this revival, which I must not omit to mention. When I was on my way to Rochester, as we passed through a village, some thirty miles east of Rochester, a brother minister whom I knew, seeing me on the

---

[53] *Ch. 12.* Note the lesson here of persevering and wrestling in prayer as a necessary ingredient for having a successful prayer life. Paul told the Colossians that Epaphras was "always laboring fervently for you in prayers (4:12)". The Greek word for "laboring fervently" is *agonizomai* and it means to struggle, to compete for a prize (in a literal sense), contend with an adversary (in a figurative sense), and is translated elsewhere as to "fight" and to "strive". Our English word *agonize* is derived from this Greek word. Like Jacob who wrestled with God and refused to stop until he received a blessing (Gen 32:22-30) we must be willing to agonize in prayer, wrestling with God and not give up until we receive the blessing that we are praying for.

canalboat, jumped aboard to have a little conversation with me, intending to ride but a little way and return. He, however, became interested in conversation, and upon finding where I was going, he made up his mind to keep on and go with me to Rochester. We had been there but a few days when this minister became so convicted that he could not help weeping aloud, at one time, as he passed along the street. The Lord gave him a powerful spirit of prayer, and his heart was broken. As he and I prayed much together, I was struck with his faith in regard to what the Lord was going to do there. I recollect he would say, "Lord, I do not know how it is; but I seem to know that thou art going to do a great work in this city." The spirit of prayer was poured out powerfully, so much so, that some persons stayed away from the public services to pray, being unable to restrain their feelings under preaching.[54]

---

[54] *Ch. 21.* Finney indicated in his *Memoirs* that, just as the brother had prophesied, "the moral aspect of things was greatly changed by this revival. It was a young city, full of thrift and enterprise, and full of sin. The inhabitants were intelligent and enterprising, in the highest degree; but as the revival swept through the town, and converted the great mass of the most influential people, both men and women, the change in the order, sobriety, and morality of the city was wonderful (*Ch. 21*)." Peter indicated that there had been "prophets since the world began (Ac 3:21)" so it should not surprise us that there have been men and women in more modern times who have had experiences that resembled the New Testament use of this gift.

Chapter 5

Slain In The Spirit

Finney recorded several instances of what would be termed in modern times as "slain in the Spirit". However, Finney's experiences differed from most modern day accounts. Modern day accounts *usually* involve about eight characteristics that Finney's did not.

CHARLES FINNEY'S ENCOUNTERS	MODERN DAY ENCOUNTERS
Finney *did not build up an atmosphere of expectation* for this to happen	The pastor *builds up an atmosphere of expectation* for this to happen
Finney *was not encouraging* this to happen	The pastor *is encouraging* this to happen
There is *strong conviction* associated with the occurrences	There is *little or no conviction* associated with the occurrences
The person(s) experiencing this *were not expecting* this to occur	The person(s) experiencing this *are expecting* this to occur
The person(s) experiencing this *were not seeking* for this to occur	The person(s) experiencing this *are seeking* for this to occur

The person(s) experiencing this have a tendency to *become* Christians	The person(s) experiencing this have a tendency to *already be* Christians
The person(s) *did not use any mind techniques* to achieve this	The person(s) *use clearing of the mind, etc.* to achieve this experience
Finney *did not claim or pretend to have the ability* to cause persons to experience this. He never "waved his hand" or used any other means like that to try and cause it to happen	The pastor *claims to have the ability* to cause this to happen and will "wave his hands" toward the congregation or blow on them to make it happen, etc.

Finney's examples of slain in the Spirit appear to be the result of individuals becoming overwhelmed with an understanding of the way that God viewed their sinfulness. This view was so overpowering for some that they either fainted or fell to the ground.[55] The Bible makes reference to persons whose mental reactions to God resulted in trembling,[56] feelings of horror and dread,[57] becoming sick,[58] crying out,[59] panting,[60] and fainting.[61] The preaching

---

[55] The falling to the ground would have been for one of two reasons, either due to weakness induced by the view of their sinfulness or out of a strong desire to display submission towards God by falling down before Him.

[56] Psalm 119:120; Ezra 10:9; Isaiah 66:2, 5; Habakkuk 3:16

[57] Genesis 15:12

[58] Daniel 8:27

[59] Psalm 84:2

[60] Psalms 38:10

[61] Daniel 8:27, 10:7-11. Compare also Psalms 84:2, 119:81.

in the New Testament had the effect of striking people in a strong way emotionally. Peter and Stephen's sermons "cut to the heart"[62] and Paul's preaching caused fear and trembling.[63] The Scriptures indicate that the spirit and soul are somehow connected[64] so it should not surprise us that when a person is awakened spiritually that they are also affected emotionally.

Examples Of Slain In The Spirit

I had taken no thought with regard to a text upon which to preach; but waited to see the congregation. As soon as I had done praying, I arose from my knees and said: "Up, get you out of this place; for the Lord will destroy this city."[65] I told them I did not recollect where that text was; but I told them very nearly where they would find it, and then went on to explain it...As soon as I had finished the narrative, I turned upon them and said, that I understood that they had never had a religious meeting in that place; and that therefore I had a right to take it for granted, and was compelled to take it for granted, that they were an ungodly people. I pressed that home upon them with more and more energy, with my heart full almost to bursting.

I had not spoken to them in this strain of direct application, I should think, more than a quarter of an hour, when all at once an awful solemnity seemed to settle down upon them; <u>the congregation began to fall from their seats in every direction, and cried for mercy</u>. If I had had a sword in each hand, I could not have cut them off their seats as fast as they fell. Indeed <u>nearly the whole</u>

---

[62] Acts 2:37, 5:33, 7:54

[63] Acts 24:24-25

[64] Hebrews 4:12

[65] Genesis 19:14

31

congregation were either on their knees or prostrate, I should think, in less than two minutes from this first shock that fell upon them. Every one prayed for himself, who was able to speak at all.[66]

A few years before, there had been a revival there under the labors of the Methodists. It had been attended with a good deal of excitement; and many cases had occurred of, what the Methodists call, "Falling under the power of God."[67] This the Presbyterians had resisted, and, in consequence, a bad state of feeling had arisen, between the Methodists and the Presbyterians; the Methodists accusing the Presbyterians of having opposed the revival among them because of these cases of falling. As nearly as I could learn, there was a good deal of truth in this, and the Presbyterians had been decidedly in error.

I had not preached long, before, one evening, just at the close of my sermon, I observed a man fall from his seat near the door; and the people gathered around him to take care of him. From what I saw, I was satisfied that it

---

[66] *Ch. 8*

[67] This expression amongst the Methodists appears to have originated with John Wesley, founder of the Methodist movement. In a letter to his brother Samuel dated May 10, 1739, he related that "While we were praying at a society here, on Tuesday the 1st [of May] instant, the power of God (so I call it) came so mightily among us, that one, and another, and another, fell down as thunderstruck. In that hour many that were in deep anguish of spirit, were all filled with peace and joy. Ten persons, till then in sin, doubt, and fear, found such a change, that sin had no more dominion over them; and instead of the spirit of fear, they are now filled with that of love, and joy, and a sound mind. A Quaker who stood by was very angry at them, and was biting his lips and knitting his brows, when the Spirit of God came upon him also, so that he fell down as one dead. We prayed over him, and he soon lifted up his head with joy, and joined with us in thanksgiving." See also Wesley's journal entry for May 1, 1739.

32

was a case of falling under the power of God, as the Methodists would express it, and supposed that it was a Methodist. I must say that I had a little fear that it might reproduce that state of division and alienation that had before existed. But on inquiry I learned that it was one of the principal members of the Presbyterian church, that had fallen. And it was remarkable that <u>during this revival, there were several cases of this kind among the Presbyterians</u>, and none among the Methodists. This led to such confessions and explanations among the members of the different churches, as to secure a state of great cordiality and good feeling among them.[68]

At this moment a young man by the name of W—, a clerk in Mr. H—'s store, being one of the first young men in the place, <u>so nearly fainted, that he fell upon some young men that stood near him; and they all of them partially swooned away, and fell together</u>. This had well-nigh produced a loud shrieking; but I hushed them down, and said to the young men, "Please set that door wide open, and go out, and let all retire in silence." They did as I requested. They did not shriek; but they went out sobbing and sighing, and their sobs and sighs could be heard till they got out into the street.[69]

At one of our morning prayer meetings, the lower part of the church was full. I arose and was making some remarks to the people, when an unconverted man, a merchant, came into the meeting. He came along till he found a seat in front of me, and near where I stood

-----

[68] *Ch. 11*
[69] *Ch. 13*

speaking. <u>He had sat but a few moments, when he fell from his seat as if he had been shot</u>. He writhed and groaned in a terrible manner. I stepped to the pew door, and saw that <u>it was altogether an agony of mind</u>. A skeptical physician sat near him. He stepped out of his slip, and came and examined this man who was thus distressed. He felt his pulse, and examined the case for a few moments. He said nothing, but turned away, and leaned his head against a post that supported the gallery, and manifested great agitation. He said afterward that he saw at once that <u>it was distress of mind</u>, and it took his skepticism entirely away. He was soon after hopefully converted. We engaged in prayer for <u>the man who fell in the pew</u>; and before he left the house, I believe, his anguish passed away, and he rejoiced in Christ.[70]

———————

There was the wife of an officer in the United States army residing at Rome, the daughter of a prominent citizen of that place. This lady manifested a good deal of opposition to the work, and, as was reported, said some strong things against it; and this led to her being made a particular subject of prayer. This had come to my knowledge but a short time before the event occurred, which I am about to relate. I believe, in this case, some of the principal women made this lady a particular subject of prayer, as she was a person of prominent influence in the place. She was an educated lady, of great force of character, and of strong will; and of course she made her opposition felt. But almost as soon as this was known, and the spirit of prayer was given for her in particular, the Spirit of God took her case in hand. One evening, almost immediately after I had heard of her case, and perhaps

———————

[70] *Ch. 13*

the evening of the very day that the facts came to my knowledge, after the meeting was dismissed, and the people had retired, Mr. Gillett[71] and myself had remained to the very last, conversing with some persons who were deeply bowed down with conviction. As they went away, and we were about to retire, the sexton came hurriedly to us as we were going out, and said, "There is a lady in yonder pew that cannot get out; she is helpless. Will you not come and see her?" We returned, and lo! down in the pew, was this lady of whom I have spoken, perfectly overwhelmed with conviction. The pew had been full, and she had attempted to retire with the others that went out; but as she was the last to go out, she found herself unable to stand, and sunk down upon the floor, and did so without being noticed by those that preceded her. We had some conversation with her, and found that the Lord had stricken her with unutterable conviction of sin. After praying with her, and giving her the solemn charge to give her heart immediately to Christ, I left her; and Mr. Gillett, I believe, helped her home. It was but a few rods to her house. We afterwards learned, that when she got home she went into a chamber by herself and spent the night. It was a cold winter's night. She locked herself in, and spent the night alone. The next day she expressed hope in Christ, and so far as I have known, proved to be soundly converted.[72]

Of all this, I knew nothing at the time, of course. I had been visiting and laboring with inquirers the whole day, and had had no time whatever, to arrange my

---

[71] That is, Rev. Moses Gillett (d.1848), pastor of the Congregational Church in Rome, New York.
[72] *Ch. 13*

thoughts, or even settle upon a text. During the introductory services, a text occurred to my mind. It was the words of the man with the unclean spirit, who cried out, "Let us alone."[73] I took those words and went on to preach, and endeavored to show up the conduct of those sinners that wanted to let be alone, that did not want to have anything to do with Christ.

The Lord gave me power to give a very vivid description of the course that class of men were pursuing. In the midst of my discourse, <u>I observed a person fall from his seat near the broad aisle, who cried out in a most terrific manner</u>. The congregation were very much shocked; and the outcry of the man was so great, that I stopped preaching and stood still. After a few moments, I requested the congregation to sit still, while I should go down and speak with the man. I found him to be this Mr. E—, of whom I have been speaking. <u>The Spirit of the Lord had so powerfully convicted him, that he was unable to sit on his seat</u>. When I reached him, he had so far recovered his strength as to be on his knees, with his head on his wife's lap. He was weeping aloud like a child confessing his sins, and accusing himself in a terrible manner. I said a few words to him, to which he seemed to pay but little attention. The Spirit of God had his attention so thoroughly, that I soon desisted from all efforts to make him attend to what I said. When I told the congregation who it was, they all knew him and his character; and it produced tears and sobs in every part of the house. I stood for some little time, to see if he would be quiet enough for me to go on with my sermon; but his loud weeping rendered it impossible. I can never forget the appearance of his wife, as she sat and held his face in

---

[73] Mark 1:24

her hands upon her lap. There appeared in her face a holy joy and triumph that words cannot express.[74]

––––––––––

The spirit of prayer in the meantime had come powerfully upon me, as had been the case for some time with Miss S—. The praying power so manifestly spreading and increasing, the work soon took on a very powerful type; so much so that <u>the word of the Lord would cut the strongest men down, and render them entirely helpless</u>. I could name many cases of this kind.

One of the first that I recollect was on Sabbath, when I was preaching on the text, "God is love."[75] There was a man by the name of J—, a man of strong nerves, and of considerable prominence as a farmer, in the town. He sat almost immediately before me, near the pulpit. The first that <u>I observed was that he fell, and writhed in agony for a few moments; but afterwards became still, and nearly motionless, but entirely helpless</u>. He remained in this state until the meeting was out, when he was taken home. He was very soon converted, and became an effective worker, in bringing his friends to Christ.[76]

––––––––––

Among other conversions I must not forget to mention that of Mr. P—, a prominent citizen of that place, a bookseller. Mr. P— was an infidel; not an atheist, but a disbeliever in the divine authority of the Bible. He was a reader and a thinker, a man of keen, shrewd mind, strong will, and most decided character. He was, I believe, a man of good outward morals, and a gentleman highly

––––––––––

[74] *Ch. 15*
[75] 1John 4:8
[76] *Ch. 17*

respected. He came to my room early one morning, and said to me, "Mr. Finney, there is a great movement here on the subject of religion, but I am a skeptic, and I want you to prove to me that the Bible is true." The Lord enabled me at once to discern his state of mind, so far as to decide the course I should take with him. I said to him, "Do you believe in the existence of God?"

"O yes!" he said, "I am not an atheist."

"Well, do you believe that you have treated God as you ought? Have you respected his authority? Have you loved him? Have you done that which you thought would please him, and with the design to please him? Don't you admit that you ought to love him, and ought to worship him, and ought to obey him, according to the best light you have?"

"O yes!" he said, "I admit all this."

"But have you done so?" I asked.

"Why, no," he answered, "I cannot say that I have."

"Well then," I replied, "why should I give you farther information, and farther light, if you will not do your duty and obey the light you already have?" "Now," said I, "when you will make up your mind to live up to your convictions, to obey God according to the best light you have; when you will make up your mind to repent of your neglect thus far, and to please God just as well as you know how, the rest of your life, I will try to show you that the Bible is from God. Until then it is of no use for me to do any such thing." I did not sit down, and I think had not asked him to sit down. He replied, "I do not know but that is fair;" and retired.

I heard no more of him until the next morning. Soon after I arose, he came to my room again; and as soon as he entered, he clapped his hands and said, "Mr. Finney, God has wrought a miracle!" "I went down to the store," he continued, "after I left your room, thinking of what you had said; and I made up my mind that I would repent of what I knew was wrong in my relations to God, and that hereafter I would live according to the best light I had. And when I made up my mind to this," said he, "<u>my feelings so overcame me that I fell</u>; and I do not know but I should have died, if it had not been for Mr.—, who was with me in the store." From this time he has been, as all who know him are aware, a praying, earnest Christian man. For many years he has been one of the trustees of Oberlin College, has stood by us through all our trials, and has aided us with his means and his whole influence.[77]

Charles Finney's Understanding
Of The Slain In The Spirit Phenomena

The following article is from a series of letters that Finney originally wrote for a New York based periodical entitled *The Independent* between 1845 and 1846. Some of these letters were later compiled into a book entitled *Revival Fire*. In the excerpt that follows Finney attempts to offer an explanation for why persons sometimes pass out in church meetings and also makes a distinction between true experiences induced by the Holy Spirit and emotionally induced "slain the Spirit" experiences.

I have by no means done with the subject of excitement as connected with revivals of religion. In every age of the Church, cases have occurred in which persons have had such clear manifestations of Divine truth as to prostrate their physical strength entirely. This appears to have been the case with Daniel. He fainted and was

---

[77] *Ch. 21*

unable to stand. Saul of Tarsus seems to have been overwhelmed and prostrated under the blaze of Divine glory that surrounded him. I have met with many cases where the physical powers were entirely prostrated by a clear apprehension of the infinitely great and weighty truths of religion.

With respect to these cases I remark:

1 That they are not cases of that objectionable excitement of which I spoke in my former letter. For in these cases, the intelligence does not appear to be stultified and confused, but to be full of light. The mind seems not to be conscious of any unusual excitement of its own sensibility; but, on the contrary, seems to itself to be calm, and its state seems peculiar only because truth is seen with unusual clearness. Manifestly there is no such effervescence of the sensibility as produces tears, or any of the usual manifestations of an excited imagination, or deeply moved feelings. There is not that gush of feeling which distracts the thoughts; but the mind sees truth, unveiled, and in such relations as really to take away all bodily strength, while the mind looks in upon the unveiled glories of the Godhead. The veil seems to be removed from the mind, and truth is seen much as we must suppose it to be when the spirit is disembodied. No wonder this should overpower the body.

Now such cases have often stumbled those who have witnessed them; and yet, so far as I have had opportunity to inquire into their subsequent history, I have been persuaded that, in general, these were sound cases of conversion. A few may possibly be counterfeits; but I do not recollect any clearly marked case of this kind in which it was not afterwards manifest that the love of God had been deeply shed abroad in the heart, the will greatly subdued, and the whole character greatly and most desirably modified.

Now, I again remark that I do not feel at liberty to object to these cases of excitement, if they may be so called. Whatever excitement attends them seems to result necessarily from the clear manifestations which God makes to the soul. This excitement, instead of being boisterous, unintelligent, and enthusiastic, like that alluded to in my former letter, seems to be similar to that which we may suppose exists among the departed spirits of the just. Indeed, this seems to me a just principle: We need fear no kind or degree of excitement which is produced simply by perceived truth, and is consistent with the healthful operation of the intellectual powers. Whatever exceeds this, must be disastrous.

In general, those cases of bodily prostration of which I have spoken occur without the apparent intervention of any external means adapted to produce such a result. So far as I have observed, they occur when the soul is shut up to God. In the case of Daniel, of Saul, of William Tennant,[78] and others, there were no human instrumentalities, or measures, or exciting appeals to the imagination or sensibility; but a simple revelation of God to the soul by the Holy Ghost.

Now the excitement produced in this manner seems to be of a very different kind from that produced by very

---

[78] William Tennant (1673-1746), sometimes spelled Tennent, was a Presbyterian minister who went into an unconscious state for three days during which he was thought to have died. During his time of unconsciousness he experienced a vision of heaven. For more details on Tennant see Elias Boudinot's *Life Of The Rev. William Tennent, Formerly Pastor Of The Presbyterian Church At Freehold, New Jersey.—In Which Is Contained, Among Other Interesting Particulars, An Account Of His Being Three Days In A Trance, And Apparently Lifeless* (New York: Robert Carter, 1848).

boisterous, vociferous preaching, exhortation or prayer; or by those very exciting appeals to fear which are often made by zealous exhorters or preachers. Exciting measures are often used, and very exciting illustrations are employed, which agitate and strain the nervous system until the sensibility seems to gush forth like a flood of water, and for the time completely overwhelm and drown the intelligence.

But the excitement produced when the Holy Ghost reveals God to the soul is totally different from this. It is not only consistent with the clearest and most enlarged perceptions of the intelligence, but directly promotes and produces such perceptions. Indeed, it promotes the free and unembarrassed action of both the intelligence and the will.

This is the kind of excitement that we need. It is that which the Holy Spirit always produces. It is not an excitement of sympathy; not a spasm, or explosion of the nervous sensibility; but is a calm, deep, sacred flow of the soul in view of the clear, infinitely important, and impressive truths of God.

It requires, often, no little discrimination to distinguish between an effervescence of the sensibility produced by loud and exciting appeals — by corresponding measures, on the one hand; and, on the other, that calm, but deep, and sometimes over-powering flow of soul which is produced by the Spirit of God, revealing Jesus to the soul. I have sometimes feared that these different kinds of excitement are confounded with each other, and consequently, by one class of persons, all alike rejected and denounced; and by another class, wholly defended. Now it appears to me of great importance to distinguish in these cases between things that differ.

When I see cases of extraordinary excitement, I have learned to inquire, as calmly and affectionately as I can, into the views of truth taken by the mind at the time. If the individual readily and spontaneously gives such reasons as naturally account for this excitement, I can then judge of its character. If it really originates in clear views presented by the Holy Ghost, of the character of God and of the great truths of His government, the mind will be full of these truths, and will spontaneously give them off whenever there is ability to utter them. It will be seen that there is a remarkably clear view of truth, and, where power of speech is left, a remarkable facility in communicating it. As a general thing, I do not fear the excitement in these cases.

But where the attention seems to be occupied with one's own feelings, and when they can give no intelligible reason for feeling as they do, very little confidence can be placed in their state. I have frequently seen cases when the excitement was very great, and almost overwhelming; yet the subject of it, upon the closest inquiry, could give no intelligent account of any perceptions of truth which the mind had. The soul seemed to be moved to its deepest foundations; but not by clear exhibitions of truth, or by manifestations of God to the soul. Hence the mind did not seem to be acting intelligently. I have learned to be afraid of this, and to place little or no confidence in professed conversions under such circumstances. I have observed that the subjects of these excitements will, after a season, look upon themselves as having been infatuated and swept away by a tornado of unintelligent excitement.[79]

---

[79] Finney, Charles G. *Revival Fire* (Cincinnati, OH: God's Revivalist Office, 184?), *Letter 6: Excitement In Revivals.* This letter originally

43

Arthur and Lewis Tappan, wealthy Christian businessmen who financially supported the ministry of Finney

appeared in *The Oberlin Evangelist*, May 7, 1845 referred to as *Letter 8* in that issue.

Chapter 6

Sinners Struck Dead

ALL

Before the very first human sin had ever been committed God warned the world that sin brings with it death.[80] Thousands of years later the apostle Paul would reinforce this to the Roman Christians by reminding them that "the wages of sin is death."[81] For some, this judgment of death is prolonged but for others it strikes sooner than later, in some cases immediately. The Scriptures make numerous references to God punishing those who resisted His plan and purpose by striking them dead. Balaam,[82] Saul,[83] Joash,[84] an unnamed prophet,[85] Ahab,[86] Jezebel,[87] members of the Assyrian resettlement program,[88] Sennacherib,[89] Amon,[90] Belshazzar,[91] Ananias, Sapphira,[92] King Herod[93], and the Corinthian church members who partook of the Lord's Supper unworthily[94] all serve as examples of men and women who resisted God's will and

---

[80] Genesis 2:17
[81] Romans 6:23
[82] Deuteronomy 23:3-5; Joshua 13:22
[83] 1Chronicles 10:13-14
[84] 2Chronicles 24:20-25
[85] 1Kings 13:1-30
[86] 1Kings 16:28-30, 2Ch 18:18-34
[87] 2Kings 9:30-37
[88] 2Kings 17:24-26
[89] 2Kings 19:20-37
[90] 2Kings 21:19-23
[91] Daniel 5:1-31
[92] Acts 5:1-11
[93] Acts 12:1-23
[94] 1Corinthians 11:17-32

died as a result. Finney also witnessed several people who resisted God's will die unusual and unexpected deaths. After studying these cases one is left to ask in what way(s), if any, did Finney's experiences of divine justice ending in death differ from the accounts found in the Bible?

An Opponent Of The Revival Is Struck Dead

There was one old man in this place, who was not only an infidel, but a great railer at religion. He was very angry at the revival movement. I heard every day of his railing and blaspheming, but took no public notice of it. He refused altogether to attend meeting. But in the midst of his opposition, and when his excitement was great, while sitting one morning at the table, he suddenly fell out of his chair in a fit of apoplexy. A physician was immediately called, who, after a brief examination, told him that he could live but a very short time; and that if he had anything to say, he must say it at once. He had just strength and time, as I was informed, to stammer out, "Don't let Finney pray over my corpse." This was the last of his opposition in that place.[95]

A Man Who Ridicules And Resists The Revival Dies Suddenly

But in this revival, as in others that I have known, God did some terrible things in righteousness. On one Sabbath while I was there, as we came out of the pulpit, and were about to leave the church, a man came in haste to Mr. Gillett and myself, and requested us to go to a certain place, saying that a man had fallen down dead there. I was engaged in conversing with somebody, and Mr. Gillett went alone. When I was through with the conversation, I went to Mr. Gillett's house, and he soon

---

[95] *Ch. 5*

46

returned and related this fact. Three men who had been opposing the work, had met that Sabbath-day, and spent the day in drinking and ridiculing the work. They went on in this way until one of them suddenly fell dead. When Mr. Gillett arrived at the house, and the circumstances were related to him, he said, "There is no doubt but that man has been stricken down by God, and has been sent to hell." His companions were speechless. They could say nothing; for it was evident to them that their conduct had brought upon him this awful stroke of divine indignation.[96]

A Minister Who Opposes The Revival Dies

One circumstance occurred, in the midst of that revival, that made a powerful impression. The Oneida presbytery met there, while the revival was going on in its full strength. Among others there was an aged clergyman, a stranger to me, who was very much annoyed by the heat and fervor of the revival. He found the public mind all absorbed on the subject of religion; that there was prayer and religious conversation everywhere, even in the stores and other public places. He had never seen a revival, and had never heard what he heard there. He was a Scotchman, and, I believe, had not been very long in this country.

On Friday afternoon, before presbytery adjourned, he arose and made a violent speech against the revival, as it was going on. What he said, greatly shocked and grieved the Christian people who were present. They felt like falling on their faces before God, and crying to him to prevent what he had said from doing any mischief.

The presbytery adjourned just at evening. Some of the members went home, and others remained overnight. Christians gave themselves to prayer. There was a great

---

[96] *Ch. 13*

crying to God that night, that he would counteract any evil influence that might result from that speech. The next morning, this man was found dead in his bed.[97]

A Former Minister Who
Resisted The Revival Is Struck Dead

Soon after the adjournment of the convention, on the Sabbath, as I came out of the pulpit, a young lady by the name of S—, from Stephentown, was introduced to me. She asked me if I could not go up to their town and preach. I replied, that my hands were full, and that I did not see that I could. I saw her utterance was choked with deep feeling; but as I had not time to converse with her then, I went to my lodging.

Afterward I made inquiry about Stephentown, a place north of, and adjoining New Lebanon. Many years before, a wealthy individual had died, and given to the Presbyterian church in that place, a fund, the interest of which was sufficient to support a pastor. Soon after this, a Mr. B—[98], who had been a chaplain in the Revolutionary army, was settled there as pastor of the church. He remained until the church ran down, and he finally became an open infidel. This had produced a most disastrous influence in that town. He remained among them, openly hostile to the Christian religion.[99]

After he had ceased to be pastor of the church, they had had one or two ministers settled. Nevertheless, the

---

[97] *Ch. 14*

[98] That is, Rev. Aaron Jordan Booge (1751-1826) sometimes spelled Bogue.

[99] Rev. Booge is remembered as being a failure as a minister, paying more attention to worldly pursuits than his ministry. See Frank Dexter's *Biographical Sketches Of The Graduates Of Yale College With The Annals Of The College History, Vol. 3: May 1763-July 1778, p. 518-19* (Henry Holt & Co., 1903) for a brief sketch of his failed ministry career.

church declined, and the state of religion grew worse and worse; until, finally, they had left their meeting house, as so few attended meeting, and held their services on the Sabbath, in a small schoolhouse, which stood near the church...The state of things in Stephentown, now demanded that I should leave New Lebanon, and take up my quarters there. I did so. The spirit of prayer in the meantime had come powerfully upon me, as had been the case for some time with Miss S—. The praying power so manifestly spreading and increasing, the work soon took on a very powerful type; so much so that the word of the Lord would cut the strongest men down, and render them entirely helpless...The fact is, the town was in an awful state. The influence of Mr. B—, their former minister, now an infidel, had borne its legitimate fruit; and there was but very little conviction of the truth and reality of religion left, among the impenitent in that town. This meeting that I have spoken of, resulted in the conviction of nearly all that were present, I believe, at the meeting. The revival spread in that neighborhood; and I recollect that in this M— family, there were seventeen hopeful conversions.

But there were several families in the town who were quite prominent in influence, who did not attend the meetings. It seemed that they were so much under the influence of Mr. B—, that they were determined not to attend. However, in the midst of the revival, this Mr. B— died a horrible death; and this put an end to his opposition.[100]

A Sinner Puts Off Repenting And Then Dies

Among the incidents that occurred, during my short stay at Lancaster, I recall the following. One evening I

---

[100] *Ch. 17*

preached on a subject that led me to insist upon the immediate acceptance of Christ. The house was very much crowded, literally packed. At the close of my sermon I made a strong appeal to the people to decide at once; and I think I called on those whose minds were made up, and who would then accept the Savior, to rise up, that we might know who they were, and that we might make them subjects of prayer. As I learned the next day; there were two men sitting near one of the doors of the church, one of whom was very much affected under the appeal that was made, and could not avoid manifesting very strong emotion, which was observed by his neighbor. However, the man did not rise up, nor give his heart to God. I had pressed the thought upon them, that might be the last opportunity that some of them would ever have, to meet and decide this question; that in so large a congregation it was not unlikely that there were those there who would then decide their everlasting destiny, one way or the other. It was not unlikely that God would hold some of them to the decision that they then made.

After the meeting was dismissed, as I learned the next day, these two men went out together, and one said to the other, "I saw you felt very deeply under the appeals Mr. Finney made." "I did," he replied. "I never felt so before in my life; and especially when he reminded us that might be the last time we should ever have an opportunity to accept the offer of mercy." They went on conversing in this way, for some distance, and then separated, each one going to his own home. It was a dark night, and the one who had felt so deeply, and was so pressed with the conviction that he might then be rejecting his last offer, fell over the curbstone, and broke his neck. This was reported to me the next day.[101]

---

[101] *Ch. 19*

A Lukewarm Minister Dies During The Revival

In Reading there were several German churches, and one Presbyterian church. The pastor of the latter was the Rev. Dr. Greer.[102] At his request, and that of the elders of the church, I went out to labor there for a time. I soon found, however, that neither Dr. Greer, nor any of his people, had any just idea of what they needed, or what a revival really was. None of them had ever seen a revival, so far as I could learn. Besides, all revival efforts, for that winter, had been forestalled, by an arrangement to have a ball every alternate week, which was attended by many of the members of the church, one of the leading elders in Dr. Greer's church being one of the managers. I could not learn that Dr. Greer had ever said anything against this. They had no preaching during the week, and I believe no religious meetings of any kind.

When I found what the state of things was, I thought it my duty to tell Dr. Greer that those balls would very soon be given up, or I should not be allowed to occupy his pulpit; that those balls, attended by his church members, and headed by one of his elders, would not long consist with my preaching. But he said, "Go on; take your own course." I did so; and preached three times on the Sabbath, and four times, I think, during the week, for about three weeks, before I said anything about any other meetings. We had no prayer meetings, I believe, for the

---

[102] That is, John Ferguson Greer (1784-1829), also spelled as Grier. This story is interesting in that it presents a preacher who died while hosting Finney at his church. Though he allowed Finney to minister in his pulpit he was "a timid man" who "did not like to face his people, and resist the encroachments of sin as he needed to do." Perhaps the timing of his death was just a mere coincidence but it should serve as a warning to all of us that we must always speak what God tells us to speak even if people do not want to hear it.

reason that the lay members had never been in the habit of taking part in such meetings. However, on the third Sabbath, I think, I gave notice that a meeting for inquiry would be held in the lecture room, in the basement of the church, on Monday evening. I stated as clearly as possible the object of the meeting, and mentioned the class of persons that I desired to attend; inviting those, and those only, that were seriously impressed with the state of their souls, and had made up their minds to attend immediately to the subject, and desired to receive instruction on the particular question of what they should do to be saved...I think I observed that conviction was taking hold of the congregation; yet I felt doubtful how many would attend a meeting of inquirers. However, when evening came, I went to the meeting. Dr. Greer came in, and behold! the lecture room, a large one — I think nearly as large as the body of the church above, full; and on looking around Dr. Greer observed that most of the impenitent persons in his congregation were present; and among them, those who were regarded as the most respectable and influential...I opened the meeting by a short address, in which I explained to them what I wished; that is to have a few moments' conversation with each of them, and to have them state to me frankly how they felt on the subject, what their convictions were, what their determinations were, what their difficulties were...When I had spent as much time as was allowed me in personal conversation, I then went back to the desk, and gave them an address; in which, according to my custom, I summed up the results of what I had found that was interesting, in the communications that they had made to me. Avoiding all personalities, I took up the representative cases, and dissected, and corrected, and taught them...As soon as I saw that they thoroughly understood me, I called on them to kneel, and knelt myself. Dr. Greer knelt by my side, but said nothing. I presented the case in prayer to God, and held right to the point of now submitting, believing, and consecrating themselves to God. There was an awful solemnity pervading the congregation, and the stillness of death, with the exception of my own voice in prayer, and the sobs, and sighs, and weeping that were heard more or less throughout the congregation. After spreading the case before God we rose from our knees, and without saying anything farther I pronounced the blessing and dismissed them. Dr. Greer took me cordially by the hand, and smiling said, "I will see you in the morning." He went his way, and I went to my lodgings. At about eleven o'clock, I should judge, a messenger came running over to my lodgings, and called me, and said that Dr. Greer was dead. I inquired what it meant. Be said he had just retired, and was taken with a fit of apoplexy, and died immediately. He was greatly respected and beloved by his people, and I am persuaded he deserved to be. He was a man of thorough education, and I trust of earnest piety. But his theological education had not at all fitted him for the work of the ministry, that is to win souls to Christ. He was besides rather a timid man. He did not like to face his people, and resist the encroachments of sin as he needed to do. His sudden death was a great shock, and became the subject of constant conversation throughout the town.[103]

---

[103] *Ch. 19.* 1John 5:16-17 tells us that "If any man sees his brother sin a sin which does not lead unto death, he shall ask, and He shall give him life for them that do not sin unto death. There is a sin unto death: I do not say that he shall pray for it. All unrighteousness is sin: and there is a sin not unto death." I believe that the best way to interpret this passage is to understand that it is teaching that we are to pray for our brothers and sisters who backslide and commit sin. However, in some cases there are some sins

Some Of Finney's Revivals		
Place	**Number Of Converts**	**Duration***
Rome, NY	500	Twenty days
Utica, NY	500	A few weeks
Rochester, NY	100,000	One year
Auburn, NY	500	Six weeks
New York, NY	500	35-40 days
Hartford, CT	600	Unspecified number of weeks
London	1500-1600[+]	Several weeks

*As recorded in Finney's Memoirs.
[+]This was just in his first weeks at the Tabernacle. Thousands of more conversions occurred in England after this period. Conversions generally continued after Finney left an area with the revived church members and new converts focusing their energy upon soul winning.

which will cause God to strike a man or woman dead as the introduction to this chapter showed is very Scriptural. In those cases they are beyond the point of prayer being able to help and John is telling us that praying will do them no good. In that sense I believe that this passage is best understood as saying "If any man sees his brother sin a sin which does not lead unto [God striking him with physical] death, he shall ask [God to lead him to repentance while he is still alive], and He shall give him [repentance unto eternal] life for them that do not sin [a sin which leads] unto [God striking them with physical] death. There is a sin [that leads] unto [God striking a person with physical] death: I do not say that he shall pray for it. All unrighteousness is sin: and there is a sin [that does] not [lead] unto [God striking a person with physical] death."

Chapter 7

Miracles And Unusual Occurrences

The New Testament is filled with miracles and unusual occurrences. Finney, in his *Memoirs*, mentioned several incidents that were either miraculous or, at the very least, very unusual. After reading them one is left to wonder in what way(s), if any, did the miracles and unusual occurrences that Finney recorded differ from the ones recorded in the Bible?

A Woman Loses The
Power Of Speech Until She Is Saved

As the people withdrew, I observed a woman in the arms of some of her friends, who were supporting her, in one part of the house; and I went to see what was the matter, supposing that she was in a fainting fit. But I soon found that she was not fainting, but that <u>she could not speak</u>. There was a look of the greatest anguish in her face, and she made me understand that <u>she could not speak</u>. I advised the women to take her home, and pray with her, and see what the Lord would do. They informed me that she was Miss G—, sister of the well-known missionary,[104] and that she was a member of the church in good standing, and had been for several years. That evening, instead of going to my usual lodgings, I accepted an invitation, and went home with a family where I had not before stopped over night. Early in the morning I found that I had been sent for to the place where I was supposed to be, several times during the night, to visit families where there were persons under awful distress of

---

[104] That is, William Goodell (1792-1867), missionary to Turkey.

mind. This led me to sally forth among the people, and everywhere I found a state of wonderful conviction of sin and alarm for their souls.

After lying in a <u>speechless state</u> about sixteen hours, Miss G—'s mouth was opened, and a new song was given her. She was taken from the horrible pit of miry clay, and her feet were set upon a rock; and it was true that many saw it and feared.[105] It occasioned a great searching among the members of the church. She declared that she had been entirely deceived; that for eight years she had been a member of the church, and thought she was a Christian, but, during the sermon the night before, she saw that she had never known the true God; and when his character arose before her mind as it was then presented, her hope "perished," as she expressed it, "like a moth."[106] She said, such a view of the holiness of God was presented, that like a great wave it swept her away from her standing, and annihilated her hope in a moment.[107]

Divine Manifestations From God

I used to have, when I was a young Christian, many seasons of communing with God which cannot be described in words. And not unfrequently those seasons would end in an impression by my mind like this: "Go, see

---

[105] Psalm 40:2-3

[106] Job 4:19-20

[107] *Ch. 5.* Luke's Gospel tells us that Zacharias became speechless because he did not believe the Lord's message given to him through Gabriel. Later, after acknowledging the vision to be true, his mouth was immediately opened and the fear of the Lord fell upon those who lived in the vicinity of Zacharias (Lk 1:5-22, 57-65). This story seems to completely parallel the one recorded in Finney's autobiography. In what way(s), if any, did this instance of muteness differ from the New Testament account?

that thou tell no man."[108] I did not understand this at the time, and several times I paid no attention to this injunction; but tried to tell my Christian brethren what communications the Lord had made to me, or rather what seasons of communion I had with him. But I soon found that it would not do to tell my brethren what was passing between the Lord and my soul. They could not understand it. They would look surprised, and sometimes, I thought, incredulous; and I soon learned to keep quiet in regard to those divine manifestations, and say but little about them.[109]

A Woman Sees Hell As She Dies

During that revival my attention was called to a sick woman in the community, who had been a member of a Baptist church, and was well-known in the place; but people had no confidence in her piety. She was fast failing with the consumption; and they begged me to call and see her. I went, and had a long conversation with her. She told me a dream which she had when she was a girl, which made her think that her sins were forgiven. Upon that she had settled down, and no argument could move her. I tried to persuade her, that there was no evidence of her conversion, in that dream. I told her plainly that her acquaintances affirmed that she had never lived a Christian life, and had never evinced a Christian temper; and I had come to try to persuade her to give up her false hope, and see if she would not now accept Jesus Christ

---

[108] Matthew 8:4

[109] *Ch. 3.* Jesus said in John 14:21 that "He that has my commandments, and keeps them, it is he that loves me: and he that loves me shall be loved of my Father, and I will love him, and will *manifest* myself to him." James tells us to "Draw near to God, and he will draw near to you (4:8)." Sadly, people often miss out on things that God wants to reveal to them simply because they refuse to draw close to Him in prayer.

that she might be saved. I dealt with her as kindly as I could, but did not fail to make her understand what I meant. But she took great offense; and after I went away complained that I tried to get away her hope and distress her mind; that I was cruel to try to distress a woman as sick as she was, in that way — to try to disturb the repose of her mind. She died not long afterward. But her death has often reminded me of Dr. Nelson's book called, "The Cause and Cure of Infidelity." When this woman came to be actually dying, her eyes were opened; and before she left the world she seemed to have such a glimpse of the character of God, and of what heaven was, and of the holiness required to dwell there, that she shrieked with agony, and exclaimed that she was going to hell. In this state, as I was informed, she died.[110]

A Woman Supernaturally
Learns To Read After Prayer

I addressed another, a tall dignified looking woman, and asked her what was the state of her mind. She replied immediately that she had given her heart to God; and went on to say that the Lord had taught her to read, since she had learned how to pray. I asked her what she meant. She said she never could read, and never had known her letters. But when she gave her heart to God, she was greatly distressed that she could not read God's word. "But I thought," she said, "that Jesus could teach me to read; and I asked him if he would not please to teach me to read his word." Said she, "I thought when I had prayed that I could read. The children have a Testament, and I went and got it; and I thought I could read what I had heard them read." "But," said she, "I went over to the school ma'am, and asked her if I read right;

---

[110] *Ch. 5*

and she said I did; and since then," said she, "I can read the word of God for myself."

I said no more; but thought there must be some mistake about this, as the woman appeared to be quite in earnest, and quite intelligent in what she said. I took pains, afterwards to inquire of her neighbors about her. They gave her an excellent character; and they all affirmed that it had been notorious that she could not read a syllable until after she was converted. I leave this to spoke for itself; there is no use in theorizing about it. Such, I think, were the undoubted facts.[111]

The Presence Of God Is
So Strong That It Can Be Felt

The state of things in the village, and in the neighborhood round about, was such that no one could come into the village, without feeling awe-stricken with the impression that God was there, in a peculiar and wonderful manner. As an illustration of this, I will relate an incident. The sheriff of the county resided in Utica. There were two courthouses in the county, one at Rome, and the other at Utica; consequently the sheriff B— by name, had much business at Rome. He afterwards told me that he had heard of the state of things at Rome[112]; and he, together with others, had a good deal of laughing, in the hotel where he boarded, about what they had heard.

But one day it was necessary for him to go to Rome. He said that he was glad to have business there; for he wanted to see for himself what it was that people talked so much about, and what the state of things really

---

[111] *Ch. 6.* If God could give people the ability to preach in languages that they had never studied (Ac 2:1-12) why should we marvel that God could give someone the ability read in a language that they had never studied?

[112] That is, in regards to the revival that was occurring there.

was in Rome. He drove on in his one horse sleigh, as he told me, without any particular impression upon his mind at all, until he crossed what was called the old canal, a place about a mile, I think, from the town. He said as soon as he crossed the old canal, a strange impression came over him, an awe so deep that he could not shake it off. He felt as if God pervaded the whole atmosphere. He said that this increased the whole way, till he came to the village. He stopped at Mr. F—'s hotel, and the hostler came out and took his horse. He observed, he said, that the hostler looked just as he himself felt, as if he were afraid to speak. He went into the house, and found the gentleman there with whom he had business. He said they were manifestly all so much impressed, they could hardly attend to business. He said that several times, in the course of the short time he was there, he had to rise from the table abruptly, and go to the window and look out, and try to divert his attention, to keep from weeping. He observed, he said, that everybody else appeared to feel just as he did. Such an awe, such a solemnity, such a state of things, he had never had any conception of before. He hastened through with his business, and returned to Utica; but, as he said, never to speak lightly of the work at Rome again. A few weeks later, at Utica, he was hopefully converted; the circumstances of which I shall relate in the proper place...The hotel at which he boarded, was at that time kept by a Mr. S—. The Spirit took powerful hold in that house. Mr. S— himself, was soon made a subject of prayer, and became converted; and a large number of his family and of his boarders. Indeed that largest hotel in the town became a center of spiritual influence, and many were converted there. The stages, as they passed through, stopped at the hotel; and so powerful was the impression in the community, that I heard of several cases of persons that just stopped for a meal, or to spend a night, being powerfully convicted and converted before they left the town. Indeed, both in this place and in Rome, it was a common remark that nobody could be in the town, or pass through it, without being aware of the presence of God; that a divine influence seemed to pervade the place, and the whole atmosphere to be instinct with a divine life.[113]

Insanity Healed

There were a great many interesting cases of conversion in this place; and there were two very striking cases of instantaneous recovery from insanity during this revival. As I went into meeting in the afternoon of one Sabbath, I saw several ladies sitting in a pew, with a woman dressed in black who seemed to be in great distress of mind; and they were partly holding her, and preventing her from going out. As I came in, one of the ladies came to me and told me that she was an insane woman; that she had been a Methodist, but had, as she supposed, fallen from grace; which had led to despair, and finally to insanity. Her husband was an intemperate man, and lived several miles from the village; and he had brought her down and left her at meeting, and had himself gone to the tavern. I said a few words to her; but she replied that she must go; that she could not hear any praying, or preaching, or singing; that hell was her portion, and she could not endure anything that made her think of heaven.

I cautioned the ladies, privately, to keep her in her seat, if they could, without her disturbing the meeting. I then went into the pulpit and read a hymn. As soon as the singing began, she struggled hard to get out. But the

---

[113] *Ch. 13, 14*

61

ladies obstructed her passage; and kindly but persistently prevented her escape. After a few moments she became quiet; but seemed to avoid hearing or attending at all to the singing. I then prayed. For some little time I heard her struggling to get out; but before I had done she became quiet, and the congregation was still. The Lord gave me a great spirit of prayer, and a text; for I had no text settled upon before. I took my text from Hebrews: "Let us come boldly unto the throne of grace, that we may obtain mercy and find grace to help in time of need."[114]

My object was to encourage faith, in ourselves, and in her; and in ourselves for her. When I began to pray, she at first made quite an effort to get out. But the ladies kindly resisted, and she finally sat still, but held her head very low, and seemed determined not to attend to what I said. But as I proceeded she began gradually to raise her head, and to look at me from within her long black bonnet. She looked up more and more until she sat upright, and looked me in the face with intense earnestness. As I proceeded to urge the people to be bold in their faith, to launch out, and commit themselves with the utmost confidence to God, through the atoning sacrifice of our great High Priest, all at once she startled the congregation by uttering a loud shriek. She then cast herself almost from her seat, held her head very low, and I could see that she "trembled very exceedingly."[115] The ladies in the pew with her, partly supported her, and watched her with manifest prayerful interest and sympathy. As I proceeded she began to look up again, and soon sat upright, with face wonderfully changed, indicating triumphant joy and peace. There was such a glow upon her countenance as I have seldom seen in any

---

[114] Hebrew 4:16
[115] Genesis 27:33

human face. Her joy was so great that she could scarcely contain herself till meeting was over; and then she soon made everybody understand around her, that she was set at liberty. She glorified God, and rejoiced with amazing triumph. About two years after, I met with her, and found her still full of joy and peace.[116]

The other case of recovery was that of a woman who had also fallen into despair and insanity. I was not present when she was restored; but was told that it was almost or quite instantaneous, by means of a baptism of the Holy Spirit.[117]

Prayer That Moves Reality

One Saturday, just before evening, a German merchant tailor, from Ogdensburgh, by the name of F—, called on me, and informed me that Squire F— had sent him from Ogdensburgh, to take my measure for a suit of clothes. I had begun to need clothes, and had once, not long before, spoken to the Lord about it, that my clothes were getting shabby; but it had not occurred to me again.[118]

Prayer Brings A Snowstorm
That Deters Opponents Of The Revival

---

[116] I have wondered if this was really a case of demon possession that was never realized as such. It involved a woman who had become insane and showed a strong aversion to prayer, preaching and singing. When the congregational singing began she "struggled hard" to get out of the service. At one point she yelled out a "loud shriek" after which she began to function as mentally normal. This behavior is reminiscent of the way that demoniacs sometimes act during their deliverance sessions. Compare this with persons in the New Testament whose demon possession resulted in insanity (Mk 5:3-6, Lk 8:27) and the deliverance of which resulted in the persons shrieking loudly (Mk 1:26, 9:26, Ac 8:7).

[117] Ch. 8

[118] Ch. 11

The presbytery of Columbia had a meeting, somewhere within its bounds, while I was at New Lebanon; and being informed that I was laboring in one of their churches, they appointed a committee to visit the place, and inquire into the state of things; for they had been led to believe, from Troy and other places, and from the opposition of Mr. Nettleton[119] and the letters of Dr. Beecher[120], that my method of conducting revivals was so very objectionable, that it was the duty of presbytery to inquire into it. They appointed two of their number, as I afterward understood, to visit the place; and they attempted to do so. As I afterward learned, though I do not recollect to have heard it at the time, the news reached New Lebanon, of this action of the presbytery, and it was feared that it might create some division, and make some disturbance, if this committee came. Some of the most engaged Christians made this a particular subject of prayer; and for a day or two before the time when they were expected, they prayed much that the Lord would overrule this thing, and not suffer it to divide the church, or introduce any element of discord. The committee were expected to be there on the Sabbath, and attend the meetings. But the day before, a violent snowstorm set in; and the snow fell so deep that they found it impossible to get through, were detained over the Sabbath, and on Monday, found their way back to their own congregations. Those brethren were the Rev. J— B—[121] and the Rev. Mr. C—[122]. Mr. C— was pastor of the Presbyterian church at Hudson, New York; and Mr.

---

[119] That is, Asahel Nettleton (1783-1844), a very successful evangelist and contemporary of Finney's who became one of his critics.

[120] That is, Lyman Beecher (1775-1863), a critic of Finney who later cooperated with him on a revival in Boston, Massachusetts.

[121] That is, Joel Tyler Benedict (1772-1833).

[122] That is, William Chester (1795-1865).

B— was pastor of the Presbyterian church in Chatham, a village some fifteen or sixteen miles below Albany.[123]

Amazing Prayer

I should say a few words in regard to the spirit of prayer which prevailed at Rome at this time. I think it was on the Saturday that I came down from Western to exchange with Mr. Gillett, that I met the church in the afternoon in a prayer meeting, in their house of worship. I endeavored to make them understand that God would immediately answer prayer, provided they fulfilled the conditions upon which he had promised to answer prayer; and especially if they believed, in the sense of expecting him to answer their requests. I observed that the church were greatly interested in my remarks, and their countenances manifested an intense desire to see an answer to their prayers. Near the close of the meeting I recollect making this remark. "I really believe, if you will unite this afternoon in the prayer of faith to God, for the immediate outpouring of his Spirit, that you will receive an answer from heaven, sooner than you would get a message from Albany, by the quickest post that could be sent."

I said this with great emphasis, and felt it; and I observed that the people were startled with my expression of earnestness and faith in respect to an

---

[123] *Ch. 16.* In Acts 12:1-19 Peter had been arrested and the church began to pray for him without ceasing. In response God supernaturally rescued him from jail. In what way(s), if any, does the miraculous prevention of these opponents of the revival after the church started praying differ from Peter's miraculous escape? Is it not the same God who rescued Peter in response to the church's prayers who also prevented these opponents from coming in response to the church's prayers? Since it is the same God is it unreasonable to believe that He would answer prayers now in the same way that He has in the past?

immediate answer to prayer. The fact is, I had so often seen this result in answer to prayer, that I made the remark without any misgiving. Nothing was said by any of the members of the church at the time; but I learned after the work had begun, that three or four members of the church called in at Mr. Gillett's study, and felt so impressed with what had been said about speedy answers to prayer, that they determined to take God at his word, and see whether he would answer while they were yet speaking.

One of them told me afterwards that they had wonderful faith given them by the Spirit of God, to pray for an immediate answer; and he added, "The answer did come quicker than we could have got an answer from Albany, by the quickest post we could have sent."[124]

A Woman Lives By Faith And
Experiences God's Miraculous Provision

I found in Syracuse a Christian woman whom they called "Mother Austin," a woman of most remarkable faith. She was poor, and entirely dependent upon the charity of the people for subsistence. She was an uneducated woman, and had been brought up manifestly in a family of very little cultivation. But she had such faith as to secure the confidence of all who knew her. The conviction seemed to be universal among both Christians and unbelievers, that mother Austin was a saint. I do not think I ever witnessed greater faith in its simplicity than was manifested by that woman. A great many facts were related to me respecting her, that showed her trust in God, and in what a remarkable manner God provided for her wants from day to day. She said to me on one occasion, "Brother Finney, it is impossible for me to suffer

---

[124] *Ch. 13*

for any of the necessaries of life, because God has said to me, 'Trust in the Lord and do good: so shalt thou dwell in the land, and verily thou shalt be fed.'"[125] She related to me many facts in her history, and many facts were related to me by others, illustrative of the power of her faith.

She said, one Saturday evening a friend of hers, but an impenitent man, called to see her; and after conversing awhile he offered her, as he went away, a five dollar bill. She said that she felt an inward admonition not to take it. She felt that it would be an act of self-righteousness on the part of that man, and might do him more harm than it would do her good. She therefore declined to take it, and he went away. She said she had just wood and food enough in the house to last over the Sabbath, and that was all; and she had no means whatever of obtaining any more. But still she was not at all afraid to trust God, in such circumstances, as she had done for so many years.

On the Sabbath day there came a violent snowstorm. On Monday morning the snow was several feet deep, and the streets were blocked up so that there was no getting out without clearing the way. She had a young son that lived with her, the two composing the whole family. They arose in the morning and found themselves snowed in, on every side. They made out to muster fuel enough for a little fire, and soon the boy began to inquire what they should have for breakfast. She said, "I do not know, my son; but the Lord will provide." She looked out, and nobody could pass the streets. The lad began to weep bitterly, and concluded that they should freeze and starve to death. However, she said she went on and made such preparations as she could, to provide for breakfast, if any should come. I think she said

---

[125] Psalm 37:3

she set her table, and made arrangements for her breakfast, believing that some would come in due season. Very soon she heard a loud talking in the streets, and went to the window to see what it was, and beheld a man in a single sleigh, and some men with him shoveling the snow so that the horse could get through. Up they came to her door, and behold! they had brought her a plenty of fuel and provision, everything to make her comfortable for several days. But time would fail me to tell the instances in which she was helped in a manner as striking as this. Indeed, it was notorious through the city, so far as I could learn, that Mother Austin's faith was like a bank; and that she never suffered for want of the necessaries of life, because she drew on God.[126]

Relying On The Holy Spirit To Give Him Sermons

I have spoken of my method of preparing for the pulpit in more recent years. When I first began to preach, and for some twelve years of my earliest ministry, I wrote not a word; and was most commonly obliged to preach without any preparation whatever, except what I got in prayer.

Oftentimes I went into the pulpit without knowing upon what text I should speak, or a word that I should say. I depended on the occasion and the Holy Spirit to suggest the text, and to open up the whole subject to my mind; and certainly in no part of my ministry have I preached with greater success and power. If I did not preach from inspiration, I don't know how I did preach. It was a common experience with me, and has been during all my ministerial life, that the subject would open up to my mind in a manner that was surprising to myself. It

---

[126] *Ch. 30.* How many blessings do we miss out on in life simply because we refuse to exercise simple faith (trust) in the Lord?

seemed that I could see with intuitive clearness just what I ought to say; and whole platoons of thoughts, words, and illustrations, came to me as fast as I could deliver them. When I first began to make "skeletons,"[127] I made them after, and not before I preached. It was to preserve the outline of the thought which had been given me, on occasions such as I have just mentioned. I found when the Spirit of God had given me a very clear view of a subject, I could not retain it, to be used on any other occasion, unless I jotted down an outline of the thoughts. But after all, I have never found myself able to use old skeletons in preaching, to any considerable extent, without remodeling them, and having a fresh and new view of the subject given me by the Holy Spirit. I almost always get my subjects on my knees in prayer; and it has been a common experience with me, upon receiving a subject from the Holy Spirit, to have it make so strong an impression on my mind as to make me tremble, so that I could with difficulty write. When subjects are thus given me that seem to go through me, body and soul, I can in a few moments make out a skeleton that shall enable me to retain the view presented by the Spirit; and I find that such sermons always tell with great power upon the people.

Some of the most telling sermons that I have ever preached in Oberlin, I have thus received after the bell had rung for church; and I was obliged to go and pour them off from my full heart, without jotting down more than the briefest possible skeleton, and that sometimes not covering half the ground that I covered in my sermon.

I tell this, not boastfully, but because it is a fact, and to give the praise to God, and not to any talents of my own. Let no man think that those sermons which have

---

[127] Sermon notes.

69

been called so powerful, were productions of my own brain, or of my own heart, unassisted by the Holy Ghost. They were not mine, but from the Holy Spirit in me.[128]

A Bedridden Christian Prays For Revival
Until He Dies And Receives An Answer After Death

A pious man in the western part of this state was sick with a consumption. He was a poor man, and sick for years. An unconverted merchant in the place, had a kind heart, and used to send him now and then some things for his comfort, or for his family. He felt grateful for the kindness, but could make no return, as he wanted to do. At length he determined that the best return he could make would be to pray for his salvation; he began to pray, and his soul kindled, and he got hold of God. There was no revival there, but by and by, to the astonishment of every body, this merchant came right out on the Lord's side. The fire kindled all over the place, a powerful revival followed, and multitudes were converted.

This poor man lingered in this way for several years, and died. After his death, I visited the place, and his widow put into my hands his diary. Among other things, he says in his diary, "I am acquainted with about thirty ministers and Churches." He then goes on to set apart certain hours in the day and week to pray for each of

---

[128] *Ch. 7*. This type of preaching is even more remarkable in light of the fact that in Finney's time in New England ministers were trained at seminary to write out their entire sermons, as if it was an article, and then read it to the congregation. For a man to get up with no preparation and then preach is certainly an amazing feat in our time and, given the circumstances of how Finney's contemporary ministers prepared their sermons, it would have been viewed as even more astonishing in his day. If only ministers today would spend more time praying for their sermons than they do in writing them how different the churches of our times would be.

70

these ministers and Churches, and also certain seasons for praying for the different missionary stations. Then followed, under different dates, such facts as these: "To-day," naming the date, "I have been enabled to offer what I call the prayer of faith for the outpouring of the Spirit on — church, and I trust in God there will soon be a revival there." Under another date, "I have to-day been able to offer what I call the prayer of faith for such a church, and trust there will soon be a revival there." Thus he had gone over a great number of churches, recording the fact that he had prayed for them in faith that a revival might soon prevail among them. Of the missionary stations, if I recollect right, he mentioned in particular the mission at Ceylon. I believe the last place mentioned in his diary, for which he offered the prayer of faith, was the place in which he lived. Not long after noticing these facts in his diary, the revival commenced, and went over the region of country, nearly, I believe, if not quite, in the order in which they had been mentioned in his diary; and in due time news came from Ceylon that there was a revival of religion there. The revival in his own town did not commence till after his death. Its commencement was at the time when his widow put into my hands the document to which I have referred. She told me that he was so exercised in prayer during his sickness, that she often feared he would pray himself to death. The revival was exceedingly great and powerful in all the region; and the fact that it was about to prevail had not been hidden from this servant of the Lord...Thus this man, too feeble in body to go out of his house, was yet more useful to the world and the Church of God, than all the heartless professors in the country. Standing between God and the desolations of Zion, and pouring out his heart in believing prayer, as a prince he had power with God, and prevailed.[129]

An Agonizing Time Of Prayer
Leads To A Banker's Conversion

In this revival, as in those that had preceded, there was a very earnest spirit of prayer. We had a prayer meeting from house to house, daily, at eleven o'clock. At one of those meetings I recollect that a Mr. S—, cashier of a bank in that city, was so pressed by the spirit of prayer, that when the meeting was dismissed he was unable to rise from his knees, as we had all just been kneeling in prayer. He remained upon his knees, and writhed and groaned in agony. He said, "Pray for Mr.—," president of the bank of which he was cashier. This president was a wealthy, unconverted man.

When it was seen that his soul was in travail for that man, the praying people knelt down, and wrestled in prayer for his conversion. As soon as the mind of Mr. S— was so relieved that he could go home, we all retired; and soon after the president of the bank, for whom we prayed, expressed hope in Christ. He had not before this, I believe, attended any of the meetings; and it was not known that he was concerned about his salvation. But prayer prevailed, and God soon took his case in hand.[130]

---

[129] Genesis 32:28. *Lectures On Revivals Of Religion* 6th edition (New York: Leavitt, Lord & Co., 1835), Lecture 7: Be Filled With The Spirit, Sec. 4.10.
[130] *Ch. 16*

Chapter 8

Tears Of Repentance

The ministry of Charles Finney was noted for bringing people to tears as they came face to face with how God viewed their sinfulness. Real ministry must bring men and women to the point of sorrow for the sins that they have committed[131] and it is hoped that these examples will encourage ministers today to preach in such a manner that persons are moved to tears over their sinfulness.

In the meantime the brethren and sisters that were on their knees, began to <u>groan</u>, and <u>sigh</u>, and <u>weep</u>, and <u>agonize</u> in prayer...no one in the room could get off from his knees. They could only <u>weep</u> and confess, and all melt down before the Lord.[132]

---

[131] This is really the only way that a person can be saved. 2Corinthians 7:10 indicates that "godly sorrow causes repentance leading to salvation." If a person does not have godly sorrow over their sins they will not repent and if a man will not repent he or she can never be saved. Godly sorrow is feeling sorry for the way that our sins have affected God. People often feel sorry when they think about the punishment or consequences of their sins but this is not godly sorrow. It is selfish sorrow. They are only sorry because of what has happened or is going to happen to them because of their sin. Take for example a man who commits the crime of robbery and is caught by the police. He may feel sorrow because he is going to have to go to prison but he does not feel sorrow for how his actions have affected God and the people that he stole from. He has sorrow but it is only for himself. If a person will be saved they must develop sorrow for the way their actions have affected God and their fellow man. If they do not develop these feelings they are not saved.

[132] *Ch. 3*

While I was preaching, I observed a Methodist sister with whom I had become acquainted, and whom I regarded as an excellent Christian woman, <u>weeping</u>, as she sat near the pulpit stairs.[133]

Just before I was through, the deacon of the Presbyterian church had occasion to go out...as he went into the vestibule of the church, he found the old elder sitting there with the door ajar, and listening to what I was saying, and <u>absolutely weeping</u> himself.[134]

I was so earnest with them, that they both began to <u>weep</u>...I cast myself down upon my knees and began to pray; and they knelt down and <u>wept sorely</u>.[135]

...the church were disposed to make to the world a public confession of their backsliding, and want of a Christian spirit...a confession was drawn up...and then read before the congregation. The church arose and stood, <u>many of them weeping</u> while the confession was read.[136]

We knelt down to pray. I had not proceeded far in prayer before she began to <u>weep</u>, and to pray audibly for her husband.[137]

...he preached the borrowed sermon to his people. It was a sermon...constructed for the purpose of bringing sinners face to face with their duty to God. At the close of

---

[133] *Ch. 8*
[134] *Ch. 10*
[135] *Ch. 12*
[136] *Ch. 15*
[137] *Ch. 21*

the service he saw that many were very <u>much affected</u>, and remained in their seats <u>weeping</u>.[138]

We were scarcely seated before the son of Mr. B— came into the parlor, announcing that one of the servants was <u>deeply moved</u>. In a very short time, that one also gave evidence of submission to Christ. Then I learned that another was <u>weeping</u> in the kitchen, and went immediately to her...[139]

I led in prayer...The <u>agitation</u> deepened every moment; and as I could hear their <u>sobs</u>, and <u>sighs</u>, I closed my prayer and rose suddenly from my knees.[140]

They...went out [of the service] <u>sobbing</u> and <u>sighing</u>, and their <u>sobs</u> and <u>sighs</u> could be heard till they got out into the street.[141]

He made no reply, but cast himself across the side of the pulpit, and <u>wept like a child</u>. The congregation...almost universally dropped their heads upon the seat in front of them, and many of them <u>wept on every side</u>. With the exception of the <u>sobs</u> and <u>sighs</u>, the house was profoundly silent.[142]

There was an awful solemnity pervading the congregation, and the stillness of death, with the exception of my own voice in prayer, and the <u>sobs</u>, and

---

[138] *Ch. 29*
[139] *Ch. 35*
[140] *Ch. 13*
[141] *Ch. 13*
[142] *Ch. 15*

sighs, and weeping that were heard more or less throughout the congregation.[143]

As I was about to ask them to kneel down, and commit themselves entirely and forever to Christ, a man cried out in the midst of the congregation, in the greatest distress of mind, that he had sinned away his day of grace...there was a great sobbing and weeping in every part of the house.[144]

The people sobbed and wept all over the congregation.[145]

He listened with astonishment to what I was saying, and the first I knew he partly fell upon the floor, and cried out in the greatest agony of mind, "Do pray for me!"[146]

...almost in the midst of my discourse I saw a powerful looking man, about in the middle of the house, fall from his seat. As he sunk down he groaned, and then cried or shrieked out, that he was sinking to hell. He repeated that several times.[147]

...all at once an awful solemnity seemed to settle down upon them; the congregation began to fall from their seats in every direction, and cried for mercy...Every one prayed for himself, who was able to speak at all.[148]

---

[143] *Ch. 19*
[144] *Ch. 29*
[145] *Ch. 31*
[146] *Ch. 2*
[147] *Ch. 5*
[148] *Ch. 8*

...I was describing the manner in which some men would oppose their families, and if possible, prevent their being converted....a man <u>cried out</u> in the congregation, "Name me!" and then threw his head forward on the seat before him; and it was plain that he <u>trembled with great emotion</u>.[149]

In the midst of my discourse, I observed a person fall from his seat near the broad aisle, who <u>cried out</u> in a most terrific manner. The congregation were very much shocked; and the <u>outcry</u> of the man was so great, that I stopped preaching and stood still.[150]

After a short time I went down to...where my father lived, and visited him. He was an unconverted man...My father met me at the gate and said, "How do you do, Charles?" I replied, "I am well, father, body and soul. But, father, you are an old man; all your children are grown up and have left your house; and I never heard a prayer in my father's house." Father dropped his head, and <u>burst into tears</u>, and replied, "I know it, Charles; come in and pray yourself."[151]

When I came to dwell upon the atonement, and showed that it was made for all men...I saw his feelings rise, till at last he put both hands over his face, threw his head forward upon his knees, and <u>trembled all over with emotion</u>. I saw that the blood rushed to his head, and that the <u>tears began to flow freely</u>.[152]

---

[149] *Ch. 15*
[150] *Ch. 15*
[151] *Ch. 3*
[152] *Ch. 10*

The people waxed very mellow; and the tears flowed very freely when I held up that covenant, as still the covenant which God makes with parents and their household. The congregation was much moved and melted.[153]

When I was done, the people thronged around me on every side, and with tears thanked me for so full and satisfactory an exhibition of that subject.[154]

...the elder, who was the principal man among them, and opened the meeting, bursting into tears, exclaimed, "Brother Finney, it is all true!" He fell upon his knees and wept aloud. This was the signal for a general breaking down. Every man and woman went down upon their knees...They all wept, and confessed, and broke their hearts before God. This scene continued, I presume, for an hour...[155]

...I went into the factory, to look through it...a great number of young women were attending to their weaving, I observed a couple of them eyeing me...One of them was trying to mend a broken thread...When I came within eight or ten feet of her, I looked solemnly at her. She observed it, and was quite overcome, and sunk down, and burst into tears. The impression caught almost like powder, and in a few moments nearly all in the room were in tears. This feeling spread through the factory.[156]

The congregation were very much shocked; and the outcry of the man was so great, that I stopped preaching

---

[153] *Ch. 10*
[154] *Ch. 10*
[155] *Ch. 12*
[156] *Ch. 14*

and stood still...He was <u>weeping aloud like a child</u> confessing his sins, and accusing himself in a terrible manner...When I told the congregation who it was, they all knew him and his character; and it produced <u>tears and sobs in every part of the house</u>. I stood for some little time, to see if he would be quiet enough for me to go on with my sermon; but his <u>loud weeping</u> rendered it impossible.[157]

I felt that the Lord was answering prayer...When I stopped praying, and opened my eyes and looked at her, her face was turned up toward heaven, and the <u>tears streaming down</u>; and she was in the attitude of praying that she might be made a little child.[158]

As soon as she opened her mouth it was apparent to everybody that a great change had come over her...The ladies were greatly interested in what the old woman said...All turned and leaned toward her, to hear every word that she said, <u>the tears began to flow</u>, and a great movement of the Spirit seemed to be visible at once throughout the meeting.[159]

As I proceeded to urge the people to be bold in their faith, to launch out, and commit themselves with the utmost confidence to God, through the atoning sacrifice of our great High Priest, all at once she startled the congregation by uttering a <u>loud shriek</u>.[160]

---

[157] *Ch. 15*
[158] *Ch. 21*
[159] *Ch. 30*
[160] *Ch. 8*

She burst out into the aisle, and came forward, like a person in a state of desperation. She seemed to have lost all sense of the presence of anybody but God. She came rushing forward to the front seats, until she finally fell in the aisle, and shrieked with agony.[161]

Her countenance waxed pale, in a moment after she threw up her hands and shrieked, and then fell forward upon the arm of the sofa, and let her heart break. I think she had not wept at all before. Her eyes were dry, her countenance haggard and pale, her sensibility all locked up; but now the flood gates were opened, she let her whole gushing heart out before God.[162]

Everybody knew that what I said was true, and they quailed under it. They did not appear offended; but the people wept about as much as I did myself. I think there were scarcely any dry eyes in the house.[163]

Not unfrequently, when I brought out strongly the contrast between my own views, and the views in which they had been instructed, some laughed [in contempt], some wept, some were manifestly angry...[164]

When he came to have them before him, they were so anxious about their souls that they wept, and he saw that they were in such a state, that it very much confounded him.[165]

---

[161] *Ch. 9*
[162] *Ch. 14*
[163] *Ch. 8*
[164] *Ch. 18*
[165] *Ch. 21*

There was a great gush of feeling, in every part of the house. Many held down their heads and <u>wept</u>; others seemed to be engaged in earnest prayer.[166]

---

[166] *Ch. 26.* Compare the example of the sinful woman who anointed Jesus' feet with her tears of sorrow for her sinfulness and received forgiveness (Lk 7:36-50).

Chapter 9

Examples Of Conviction

Finney's ministry was noted for bringing *conviction* into the hearts of those whom he ministered to. Conviction is when a person's conscience convicts them of being guilty. This involves the individual mentally becoming convicted (i.e. convinced) that his or her behavior is wrong. In a church setting, it generally occurs when a minister is preaching against the sins that the listener has committed. If ministers are to be successful at their calling they must rely upon and submit to the leading of the Holy Spirit and preach in such a way as to cause their listener's to feel convicted.

References To Conviction

Soon after I was converted, the man with whom I had been boarding for some time, who was a magistrate, and one of the principal men in the place, was <u>deeply convicted</u> of sin.[167]

More or less <u>convictions</u> occurred under every sermon that I preached [at Evans' Mills]...[168]

I saw that a <u>general conviction</u> was spreading over the whole congregation.[169]

---

[167] *Ch. 3*
[168] *Ch. 5*
[169] *Ch. 5*

This led me to sally forth among the people, and everywhere I found a state of <u>wonderful conviction</u> of sin and alarm for their souls.[170]

In a very few days it was found that the whole settlement was <u>under conviction</u>; elders of the church and all were in the greatest consternation, feeling that they had no holiness.[171]

On inquiry I found that she was <u>under conviction</u> of sin, and had a most remarkably clear apprehension of her character and position before God.[172]

A man in London went home from one of our meetings <u>greatly convicted</u>.[173]

But the labors of this day were effectual to the <u>conviction</u> of the great mass of the population.[174]

His agony became intense; and as soon as the way was opened for him to speak out, he surrendered himself up to his <u>convictions</u>, and soon after expressed hope in Christ.[175]

There was a considerable number of men, and some of them prominent men, in the village, that had been under <u>strong conviction</u>, and appeared to be near conversion...[176]

---

[170] *Ch. 5*
[171] *Ch. 6*
[172] *Ch. 6*
[173] *Ch. 7*
[174] *Ch. 8*
[175] *Ch. 10*
[176] *Ch. 10*

As they arose one after another, and told what the Lord had done, and was doing, for their souls, the impression increased; and so spontaneous a movement by the Holy Ghost, in <u>convicting</u> and converting sinners, I had scarcely ever seen.[177]

I entered into conversation with her, and by God's help stripped the covering from her heart, and she was brought under <u>powerful conviction</u> for sin.[178]

I had conversed with her several times, and found her <u>deeply convicted</u>, and, indeed, almost in despair.[179]

I could see during the day that many heads were down, and that a great number of them were bowed down with <u>deep conviction</u> for sin.[180]

He shut the door, fell upon the floor, and burst out into a loud wailing, in view of his awful condition: This brought the family around him, and scattered <u>conviction among the whole of them</u>.[181]

The next morning, as soon as it was fairly day, people began to call at Mr. Gillett's, to have us go and visit members of their families, whom they represented as being under the <u>greatest conviction</u>.[182]

---

[177] *Ch. 11*
[178] *Ch. 12*
[179] *Ch. 12*
[180] *Ch. 13*
[181] *Ch. 13*
[182] *Ch. 13*

Convictions were so deep and universal, that we would sometimes go into a house, and find some in a kneeling posture, and some prostrate on the floor.[183]

Little H—, a girl perhaps eight or nine years old, was strongly convicted of sin, and her mother was greatly interested in her state of mind.[184]

...Mr. Gillett and myself had remained to the very last, conversing with some persons who were deeply bowed down with conviction.[185]

We returned, and lo! down in the pew, was this lady of whom I have spoken, perfectly overwhelmed with conviction...We had some conversation with her, and found that the Lord had stricken her with unutterable conviction of sin.[186]

Soon after the revival began in Rome, she was powerfully convicted again by the Spirit of the Lord.[187]

...I heard of several cases of persons that just stopped for a meal, or to spend a night, being powerfully convicted and converted before they left the town.[188]

This aroused her opposition; but still the work of conviction went powerfully on in her heart.[189]

---

[183] *Ch. 13*
[184] *Ch. 13*
[185] *Ch. 13*
[186] *Ch. 13*
[187] *Ch. 13*
[188] *Ch. 14*
[189] *Ch. 14*

I conversed in this strain for some time, until I saw that she was ready to sink under the <u>ripened conviction</u>...[190]

He continued the whole night in that terrible state of mind, angry, rebellious, and yet <u>so convicted that he could scarcely live</u>.[191]

It became very common under this teaching, for persons to be <u>convicted</u> and converted, in the course of a few hours, and sometimes in the course of a few minutes.[192]

Conviction So Great That A
Factory Shuts Down To Seek God

There was a cotton manufactory on the Oriskany creek, a little above Whitesboro', a place now called New York Mills. It was owned by a Mr. W—, an unconverted man, but a gentleman of high standing and good morals. My brother-in-law, Mr. G— A—, was at that time superintendent of the factory. I was invited to go and preach at that place, and went up one evening, and preached in the village schoolhouse, which was large, and was crowded with hearers. The word, I could see, took powerful effect among the people, especially among the young people who were at work in the factory.

---

[190] *Ch. 14*

[191] *Ch. 14*

[192] *Ch. 14*. These are only a portion of Finney's references to conviction (perhaps about 1/3 of the references in his autobiography are included here). I hope that it has become clear from this that a revival cannot and will not take place without conviction being at the foundation of it. When Peter preached his listeners were "pricked in their heart" and cried out "what shall we do?" (Ac 2:37). We need more preaching like this that brings with it conviction for sin. What follows are some of the more interesting examples of conviction that Finney experienced.

The next morning, after breakfast, I went into the factory, to look through it. As I went through, I observed there was a good deal of agitation among those who were busy at their looms, and their mules, and other implements of work. On passing through one of the apartments, where a great number of young women were attending to their weaving, I observed a couple of them eyeing me, and speaking very earnestly to each other; and I could see that they were a good deal agitated, although they both laughed. I went slowly toward them. They saw me coming, and were evidently much excited. One of them was trying to mend a broken thread, and I observed that her hands trembled so that she could not mend it. I approached slowly, looking on each side at the machinery, as I passed; but observed that this girl grew more and more agitated, and could not proceed with her work. When I came within eight or ten feet of her, I looked solemnly at her. She observed it, and was quite overcome, and sunk down, and burst into tears. The impression caught almost like powder, and in a few moments nearly all in the room were in tears. This feeling spread through the factory. Mr. W—, the owner of the establishment, was present, and seeing the state of things, he said to the superintendent, "Stop the mill, and let the people attend to religion; for it is more important that our souls should be saved than that this factory run."[193] The gate was immediately shut down, and the factory stopped; but where should we assemble? The superintendent suggested that the mule room was large; and, the mules being run up, we could assemble there. We did so, and a more powerful meeting I scarcely ever attended. It went on with great power. The building was large, and had many people in it, from the garret to the

---

[193] I wish that business owners today would have this mentality.

cellar. The revival went through the mill with astonishing power, and in the course of a few days nearly all in the mill were hopefully converted.[194]

Overwhelming Conviction

...on one very snowy night, when the snow had already fallen deep...I was called up about midnight, to go and visit a man who, they informed me, was under such <u>awful conviction</u> that he could not live, unless something could be done for him...He was a stalwart man, very muscular, a man of great force of will and strength of nerve, physically a fine specimen of humanity. His wife was a professor of religion; but he had "cared for none of these things."

He had been at the meeting that evening, and the sermon had torn him to pieces. He went home in a terrible state of mind, his convictions and distress increasing till it overcame his bodily strength; and his family feared he would die. Although it was in the midst of such a terrific storm, they dispatched a messenger for me. We had to face the storm, and walked perhaps fifty or sixty rods.[195] I heard his moanings, or rather howlings, before I got near the house. When I entered I found him sitting on the floor, his wife, I believe, supporting his head — and what a look in his face! It was indescribable. Accustomed as I was to seeing persons under great convictions, I must confess that his appearance gave me a tremendous shock. He was writhing in agony, grinding his teeth, and literally gnawing his tongue for pain. He cried out to me, "O, Mr. Finney! I am lost! I am a lost soul!" I was greatly shocked and exclaimed, "If this is conviction, what is hell?"

---

[194] *Ch. 14*

[195] A rod is equal to 16.5 feet. The distance would have been roughly somewhere between 800 and 1000 feet (roughly 240-300 meters).

However, I recovered myself as soon as I could, and sat down by his side. At first he found it difficult to attend; but I soon led his thoughts to the way of salvation through Christ. I pressed the Savior upon his attention and upon his acceptance. His burden was soon removed. He was persuaded to trust the Savior, and he came out free and joyful in hope.[196]

Conviction So Great That
People Have To Be Helped Home

A Mr. F—, a religious man, at that time kept a hotel, on the corner, at the center of the town. He had a large dining room; and Mr. Gitlett said, "I will step in and see if I cannot be allowed to appoint the meeting of inquiry in his dining room." Without difficulty he obtained consent, and then went immediately to the public schools, and gave notice that at one o'clock there would be a meeting of inquiry at Mr. F—'s dining room. We went home, and took our dinner, and started for the meeting. We saw people hurrying, and some of them actually running to the meeting. They were coming from every direction. By the time we were there, the room, though a large one, was crammed to its utmost capacity. Men, women, and children crowded the apartment.

This meeting was very much like the one we had had the night before. The feeling was overwhelming. Some men of the strongest nerves were so cut down by the remarks which were made, that they were unable to help themselves, and had to be taken home by their friends. This meeting lasted till nearly night. It resulted in a great number of hopeful conversions, and was the means of greatly extending the work on every side.[197]

---

[196] *Ch. 19*
[197] *Ch. 13*

Conviction That Leads To Restitution

One evening I preached on confession and restitution, and it created a most tremendous movement among business men. One man told me the next day that he had been and made restitution, I think, of fifteen hundred pounds,[198] in a case where he thought he had not acted upon the principle of loving his neighbor as himself. The consciences of men under such circumstances are exceedingly tender. The gentleman to whom I have just referred, told me that a dear friend of his had died and left him to settle his estate. He had done so, and simply received what the law gave him for his labor and expense. But he said that in hearing that sermon, it occurred to him that as a friend and a Christian brother, he could better afford to settle that estate without charging anything, than the family could afford to allow him the legal fees. The Spirit of God that was upon him led him to feel it so keenly, that he immediately went and refunded the money.[199]

A man of considerable property was converted in one of the revivals in Rochester, in which I labored, who had been transacting some business for a widow lady in a village not far distant from Rochester. The business consisted in the transfer of some real estate, for which he

---

[198] This would equal roughly $216,000.00US (£133,000GB) in 2009.

[199] *Ch. 35.* It is important to note that salvation and restitution are connected. A person who refuses to make restitution after converting cannot truly be said to have converted. In Luke 19:1-10 Zacchaeus, after cheating numerous people in the execution of his duties as a tax collector decided to restore to them four times as much as he had taken. In what way(s), if any, does the conviction of Zacchaeus differ from the conviction of today?

had been paid for his services some fifteen or sixteen hundred dollars.[200] As soon as he was converted he thought of this case; and upon reflection he thought he had not done by that widow lady and those fatherless children, as he would wish another to do by his widow and fatherless children, should he die. He therefore went over to see her, and stated to her his view of the subject as it lay before his mind. She replied that she did not see it in that light at all; that she had considered herself very much obliged to him indeed, that he had transacted her business in such a way as to make for her all she could ask or expect.

She declined, therefore, to receive the money which he offered to refund. After thinking of it a little he told her that he was dissatisfied, and wished that she would call in some of her most trustworthy neighbors, and they would state the question to them. She did so, called in some Christian friends, men of business; and they laid the whole matter before them. They said that the affair was a business transaction, and it was evident that he had transacted the business to the acceptance of the family and to their advantage; and they saw no reason why he should refund the money. He heard what they had to say; but before he left the town he called on the lady again and said, "My mind is not at ease. If I should die and leave my wife a widow and children fatherless, and a friend of mine should transact such a piece of business for them, I should feel as if he might do it gratuitously, inasmuch as it was for a widow and fatherless children." Said he, "I

---

[200] Finney had revivals in Rochester, New York, in 1830, 1842, and 1855. Depending upon which revival this took place in the value of this man's restitution would equal somewhere in between $53,000.00 and $63,000.00US (£32,600 and £38,800GB) in 2009.

cannot take any other view of it than this." Whereupon he laid the money upon her table, and left.[201]

In preaching in one of the large cities on a certain occasion, I was dwelling upon the dishonesties of business, and the overreaching plans of men; and how they justify themselves in violations of the golden rule.[202] Before I was through with my discourse, a gentleman arose in the middle of the house and asked me if he might propose a question. He then supposed a case; and after he had stated it, asked me if that case would come under the rule that I had propounded, I said, "Yes, I think that it clearly would." He sat down and said no more; but I afterwards learned that he went away and made restitution to the amount of thirty thousand dollars.[203] I could relate great numbers of instances in which persons have been led to act in the same manner, under the powerfully searching influences of the Spirit of God.[204]

Conviction Prevents A Murder

While at this place, one afternoon, a Christian brother called on me and wished me to visit his sister, who, as he informed me, was fast failing with consumption, and was a Universalist. Her husband, he said, was a Universalist, and had led her into Universalism...I went...and during my conversation with

---

[201] *Ch. 35*

[202] Matthew 7:12

[203] Finney records in his *Memoirs* having preached in large cities on at least fourteen occasions. Depending upon which year this happened in the amount would be somewhere between $973,000.00 and $1,336,000.00US (£599,000 and £823,000GB) in 2009.

[204] *Ch. 35*

her, she gave up these views entirely, and appeared to embrace the Gospel of Christ...

At evening her husband returned, and learned from herself what had taken place. He was greatly enraged, and swore he would "kill Finney." As I learned afterward, he armed himself with a loaded pistol, and that night went to meeting where I was to preach. Of this, however, I knew nothing at the time. The meeting that evening was in a schoolhouse out of the village. The house was very much packed, almost to suffocation. I went on to preach with all my might; and almost in the midst of my discourse I saw a powerful looking man, about in the middle of the house, fall from his seat. As he sunk down he groaned, and then cried or shrieked out, that he was sinking to hell. He repeated that several times...Of course this created a great excitement. It broke up my preaching; and so great was his anguish that we spent the rest of our time in praying for him.

When the meeting was dismissed his friends helped him home. The next morning I inquired for him; and found that he had spent a sleepless night, in great anguish of mind...He soon came into a state of mind that led him to indulge a hope [in Christ and of being saved]. We heard no more of his opposition.[205]

Vanity Is Overcome By Conviction

Presently a young woman came in, who had two or three tall plumes in her bonnet, and was rather gaily dressed. She was slender, tall, dignified, and decidedly handsome. I observed as soon as she came in, that she waved her head and gave a very graceful motion to her plumes. She came as it were sailing around, and up the broad aisle toward where I sat, mincing as she came, at

---

[205] *Ch. 5*

every step, waving her great plumes most gracefully, looking around just enough to see the impression she was making. For such a place the whole thing was so peculiar that it struck me very much. She entered a slip directly behind me, in which, at the time, nobody was sitting...I turned partly around, and looked at her from head to foot. She saw that I was observing her critically, and looked a little abashed. In a low voice I said to her, very earnestly "Did you come in here to divide the worship of God's house, to make people worship you, to get their attention away from God and his worship?" This made her writhe; and I followed her up, in a voice so low that nobody else heard me, but I made her hear me distinctly. She quailed under the rebuke, and could not hold up her head. She began to tremble, and when I had said enough to fasten the thought of her insufferable vanity on her mind, I arose and went into the pulpit. As soon as she saw me go into the pulpit, and that I was the minister that was about to preach, her agitation began to increase — so much so as to attract the attention of those around her. The house was soon full, and I took a text and went on to preach.

The Spirit of the Lord was evidently poured out on the congregation; and at the close of the sermon, I did what I do not know I had ever done before, called upon any who would give their hearts to God, to come forward and take the front seat. The moment I made the call, this young woman was the first to arise. She burst out into the aisle, and came forward, like a person in a state of desperation. She seemed to have lost all sense of the presence of anybody but God. She came rushing forward to the front seats, until she finally fell in the aisle, and shrieked with agony. A large number arose in different parts of the house and came forward; and a goodly number appeared to give their hearts to God upon the spot, and among them this young woman. On inquiry I found that she was rather the belle of the place; that she was an agreeable girl, but was regarded by everybody as very vain and dressy.[206]

---

[206] *Ch. 9.* These are just a few cases of conviction that Finney recorded. Indeed, his *Memoirs* could well be summed up as a record of convictions. The reader is encouraged to read the whole *Memoirs* to get a full picture of Finney's ministry.

Chapter 10

Finney's Experience With
The Baptism Of The Holy Ghost

Much interest has been shown in the last one hundred and seventy five years on the topic of the baptism of the Holy Spirit. Because Finney attributed his success as an evangelist to this baptism I felt that it would be appropriate to examine his theological understanding of it.

To fully understand how Finney interpreted the baptism of the Holy Spirit we must begin by reading his testimony of having received it. The day Finney confessed his sins to God in order to seek salvation he experienced a vision of Jesus[207] after which occurred what he described as "a mighty baptism of the Holy Ghost". His testimony is as follows:

But as I turned and was about to take a seat by the fire, I received a mighty baptism of the Holy Ghost. Without any expectation of it, without ever having the thought in my mind that there was any such thing for me, without any recollection that I had ever heard the thing mentioned by any person in the world, the Holy Spirit descended upon me in a manner that seemed to go through me, body and soul. I could feel the impression, like a wave of electricity, going through and through me. Indeed it seemed to come in waves and waves of liquid love for I could not express it in any other way. It seemed

---

[207] Finney's record of this vision appears in chapter three of this book.

96

like the very breath of God.[208] I can recollect distinctly that it seemed to fan me, like immense wings.

No words can express the wonderful love that was shed abroad in my heart.[209] I wept aloud with joy and love; and I do not know but I should say, I literally bellowed out the unutterable gushings of my heart.[210] These waves came over me, and over me, and over me, one after the other, until I recollect I cried out, "I shall die if

---

[208] Compare John 20:22.

[209] Compare Romans 5:5.

[210] Some, upon reading the phrase *"I literally bellowed out the unutterable gushings of my heart"*, have felt that Finney was here experiencing the gift of tongues as the apostles who were baptized in the Holy Spirit experienced in Acts 2. However, a close analysis of this phrase seems to indicate that this was not the meaning that Finney was trying to convey. The question here really comes down to what did he mean by the expression "bellowed out the unutterable gushings of my heart"? This event occurred in 1821. Webster's 1828 Dictionary defines "bellow" as a verb which means "To make a hollow, loud noise, as a bull; to make a loud outcry; to roar...To roar, as the sea in a tempest, or as the wind when violent; to make a loud, hollow, continued sound." He defines "unutterable" as an adjective indicating something "That cannot be uttered or expressed...inexpressible; as unutterable anguish; unutterable joy". "Gushing" he defines as "Rushing forth with violence, as a fluid; flowing copiously; as gushing waters". The experience then, of Finney having "bellowed out the unutterable gushings" of his heart, was one in which he cried out the unspeakable feelings of emotion that flow from within our heart during periods of emotional excitement—*feelings that cannot be expressed in words, but rather must be shared in groans and cries*. This understanding is in keeping with the entire phrase which indicates that "I wept aloud with joy and love; and I do not know but I should say, I literally bellowed out the unutterable gushings of my heart." The "bellowing out of the unutterable gushings of his heart" was the *way* in which Finney "wept aloud with joy and love", a loud roaring and crying out of emotion that resulted from his experience of being touched by the Holy Spirit.

these waves continue to pass over me." I said, "Lord, I cannot bear any more;" yet I had no fear of death.[211]

How long I continued in this state, with this baptism continuing to roll over me and go through me, I do not know. But I know it was late in the evening when a member of my choir — for I was the leader of the choir — came into the office to see me. He was a member of the church. He found me in this state of loud weeping, and said to me, "Mr. Finney, what ails you?" I could make him no answer for some time. He then said, "Are you in pain?" I gathered myself up as best I could, and replied, "No, but so happy that I cannot live."

He turned and left the office, and in a few minutes returned with one of the elders of the church, whose shop was nearly across the way from our office. This elder was a very serious man; and in my presence had been very watchful, and I had scarcely ever seen him laugh. When he came in, I was very much in the state in which I was when the young man went out to call him. He asked me how I felt, and I began to tell him. Instead of saying anything, he fell into a most spasmodic laughter. It seemed as if it was impossible for him to keep from laughing from the very bottom of his heart.[212]

There was a young man in the neighborhood who was preparing for college, with whom I had been very intimate. Our minister, as I afterward learned, had repeatedly talked with him on the subject of religion, and warned him against being misled by me. He informed him that I was a very careless young man about religion; and

---

[211] Compare Hebrews 2:15.

[212] I believe that God caused this to happen to show how that the Holy Spirit truly changes a person when He comes into their life. In this instance a "very serious man" of whom Finney "had scarcely ever seen him laugh" was moved to give up his seriousness.

he thought that if he associated much with me his mind would be diverted, and he would not be converted. After I was converted, and this young man was converted, he told me that he had said to Mr. Gale[213] several times, when he had admonished him about associating so much with me, that my conversations had often affected him more, religiously, than his preaching. I had, indeed, let out my feelings a good deal to this young man.

But just at the time when I was giving an account of my feelings to this elder of the church, and to the other member who was with him, this young man came into the office. I was sitting with my back toward the door, and barely observed that he came in. He listened with astonishment to what I was saying, and the first I knew he partly fell upon the floor, and cried out in the greatest agony of mind, "Do pray for me!" The elder of the church and the other member knelt down and began to pray for him; and when they had prayed, I prayed for him myself. Soon after this they all retired and left me alone.

The question then arose in my mind, "Why did Elder B— laugh so? Did he not think that I was under a delusion, or crazy?" This suggestion brought a kind of darkness over my mind; and I began to query with myself whether it was proper for me — such a sinner as I had been — to pray for that young man. A cloud seemed to shut in over me; I had no hold upon anything in which I could rest; and after a little while I retired to bed, not distressed in mind, but still at a loss to know what to make of my present state. Notwithstanding the baptism I had received, this temptation so obscured my view that I went to bed without feeling sure that my peace was made with God.

---

[213] That is, George Gale (1789-1862), Finney's pastor.

I soon fell asleep, but almost as soon awoke again on account of the great flow of the love of God that was in my heart. I was so filled with love that I could not sleep. Soon I fell asleep again, and awoke in the same manner. When I awoke, this temptation would return upon me, and the love that seemed to be in my heart would abate; but as soon as I was asleep, it was so warm within me that I would immediately awake. Thus I continued till, late at night, I obtained some sound repose. When I awoke in the morning the sun had risen, and was pouring a clear light into my room. Words cannot express the impression that this sunlight made upon me. Instantly the baptism that I had received the night before, returned upon me in the same manner. I arose upon my knees in the bed and wept aloud with joy, and remained for some time too much overwhelmed with the baptism of the Spirit to do anything but pour out my soul to God. It seemed as if this morning's baptism was accompanied with a gentle reproof, and the Spirit seemed to say to me, "Will you doubt?" "Will you doubt?" I cried, "No! I will not doubt; I cannot doubt." He then cleared the subject up so much to my mind that it was in fact impossible for me to doubt that the Spirit of God had taken possession of my soul.

In this state I was taught the doctrine of justification by faith, as a present experience. That doctrine had never taken any such possession of my mind, that I had ever viewed it distinctly as a fundamental doctrine of the Gospel. Indeed, I did not know at all what it meant in the proper sense. But I could now see and understand what was meant by the passage, "Being justified by faith, we have peace with God through our Lord Jesus Christ."[214] I could see that the moment I believed, while up in the woods all sense of condemnation had entirely dropped

---

[214] Romans 5:1

out of my mind; and that from that moment I could not feel a sense of guilt or condemnation by any effort that I could make. My sense of guilt was gone; my sins were gone; and I do not think I felt any more sense of guilt than if I never had sinned. This was just the revelation that I needed. I felt myself justified by faith; and, so far as I could see, I was in a state in which I did not sin.[215] Instead of feeling that I was sinning all the time, my heart was so full of love that it overflowed. My cup ran over with blessing and with love; and I could not feel that I was sinning against God. Nor could I recover the least sense of guilt for my past sins.[216] Of this experience I said nothing that I recollect, at the time, to anybody; that is, of this experience of justification...But now after receiving these baptisms of the Spirit I was quite willing to preach the Gospel. Nay, I found that I was unwilling to do anything else. I had no longer any desire to practice law. Everything in that direction was shut up, and had no longer any attractions for me at all. I had no disposition to make money. I had no hungering and thirsting after worldly pleasures and amusements in any direction. My whole mind was taken up with Jesus and his salvation; and the world seemed to me of very little consequence. Nothing, it seemed to me, could be put in competition with the worth of souls; and no labor, I thought, could be so sweet, and no employment so exalted, as that of holding up Christ to a dying world.[217]

This was certainly an exciting experience, both for Finney to have and for us to read about. Looking back over

---

[215] Compare 1John 3:6, 9, 5:18.

[216] Compare 2Peter 1:9.

[217] *Ch. 2, 3*

it one notices that Finney's baptism in the Holy Spirit had at least twenty distinct characteristics:

1. It happened unexpectedly[218]
2. It produced a physical feeling that Finney compared to waves (pulses?) of electricity flowing through him[219]
3. This electricity felt as if it was "liquid love" flowing through him[220]
4. It felt like wind[221]
5. It both rolled over him (the wind?) and went through him (the electricity?)[222]
6. It put a "wonderful love" into his heart[223]
7. It caused him to weep aloud with joy and love[224]
8. It was so strong that he felt that he would die if it continued[225]

---

[218] "Without any expectation of it, without ever having the thought in my mind that there was any such thing for me, without any recollection that I had ever heard the thing mentioned by any person in the world, the Holy Spirit descended upon me in a manner that seemed to go through me, body and soul."

[219] "I could feel the impression, like a wave of electricity, going through and through me."

[220] "...like a wave of electricity, going through and through me. Indeed it seemed to come in waves and waves of liquid love for I could not express it in any other way."

[221] "It seemed like the very breath of God. I can recollect distinctly that it seemed to fan me, like immense wings."

[222] "How long I continued in this state, with this baptism continuing to roll over me and go through me, I do not know."

[223] "No words can express the wonderful love that was shed abroad in my heart."

[224] "I wept aloud with joy and love; and I do not know but I should say, I literally bellowed out the unutterable gushings of my heart."

[225] "...I cried out, "I shall die if these waves continue to pass over me."

9. It took away his fear of death[226]
10. It caused a great feeling of happiness[227]
11. It affected those around him[228]
12. It was so powerful that it kept him from sleeping as normal[229]
13. It took away his doubts that he was a child of God[230]
14. It taught him the doctrine of justification by faith[231]
15. It gave him an assurance that he was living in the will of God[232]
16. It gave him the desire to preach the Gospel[233]

---

[226] "I said, "Lord, I cannot bear any more;" yet I had no fear of death."

[227] "He then said, "Are you in pain?" I gathered myself up as best I could, and replied, "No, but so happy that I cannot live.""

[228] "Instead of saying anything, he fell into a most spasmodic laughter. It seemed as if it was impossible for him to keep from laughing from the very bottom of his heart...He listened with astonishment to what I was saying, and the first I knew he partly fell upon the floor, and cried out in the greatest agony of mind, "Do pray for me!""

[229] "I soon fell asleep, but almost as soon awoke again on account of the great flow of the love of God that was in my heart. I was so filled with love that I could not sleep. Soon I fell asleep again, and awoke in the same manner. When I awoke, this temptation would return upon me, and the love that seemed to be in my heart would abate; but as soon as I was asleep, it was so warm within me that I would immediately awake. Thus I continued till, late at night, I obtained some sound repose."

[230] "It seemed as if this morning's baptism was accompanied with a gentle reproof, and the Spirit seemed to say to me, "Will you doubt?" "Will you doubt?" I cried, "No! I will not doubt; I cannot doubt." He then cleared the subject up so much to my mind that it was in fact impossible for me to doubt that the Spirit of God had taken possession of my soul."

[231] "In this state I was taught the doctrine of justification by faith, as a present experience. That doctrine had never taken any such possession of my mind, that I had ever viewed it distinctly as a fundamental doctrine of the Gospel."

[232] "I felt myself justified by faith; and, so far as I could see, I was in a state in which I did not sin."

17. It took away his desire to pursue secular success[234]
18. It took away his desire to make money[235]
19. It took away his desire for worldly pleasures and amusements[236]
20. It caused his whole mind to be taken up with the issue of Jesus, his salvation and the world's need for it[237]

Finney was left with an amazing experience but how would he theologically explain what had happened to him? Finney eventually understood his experience to be the same baptism of the Holy Spirit that the apostles received on the day of Pentecost[238]:

> The apostles and brethren, on the Day of Pentecost...received a powerful baptism of the Holy Ghost...To the honor of God alone I will say a little of *my own experience in this matter*. I was powerfully converted on the morning of the 10th of October. In the evening of the same day, and on the

---

[233] "...after receiving these baptisms of the Spirit I was quite willing to preach the Gospel. Nay, I found that I was unwilling to do anything else."

[234] "I had no longer any desire to practice law. Everything in that direction was shut up, and had no longer any attractions for me at all."

[235] "I had no disposition to make money."

[236] "I had no hungering and thirsting after worldly pleasures and amusements in any direction." Elsewhere he wrote that "Probably but few persons enjoy worldly pleasure more intensely than I did before I was converted; but my conversion, and the spiritual baptism which immediately followed it, completely extinguished all desire for worldly sports and amusements. (*Power From On High*, Ch.9 [Sussex: Victory, 1944])"

[237] "My whole mind was taken up with Jesus and his salvation...Nothing, it seemed to me, could be put in competition with the worth of souls..."

[238] Acts 2:1-41

morning of the following day, I received overwhelming baptisms of the Holy Ghost, that went through me, as it seemed to me, body and soul.[239]

Finney, however, differed from many of the modern interpretations of the baptism of the Holy Spirit in that he did not see it as a one time experience but rather as something that a Christian may experience many times over the course of their life. Even Finney himself experienced the baptism several times. On October 10, 1821, he had his first experience stating, "But as I turned and was about to take a seat by the fire, I received a mighty baptism of the Holy Ghost."[240] The next day, on October 11th, he indicated that, "Instantly the baptism that I had received the night before, returned upon me in the same manner."[241] Twenty two years later he would have another baptism of the Holy Spirit stating, "During this winter, the Lord gave my own soul a very thorough overhauling, and a fresh baptism of his Spirit."[242] These experiences would become the secret to his ministry success and his life story would be one of seeking fresh and new baptisms of the Holy Spirit:

> I was powerfully converted on the morning of the 10th of October. In the evening of the same day, and on the morning of the following day, I received overwhelming baptisms of the Holy Ghost...I immediately found myself endued with such power from on high that a few words dropped here and there to individuals were the means of their

---

[239] *Power From On High, Ch. 2*
[240] *Ch. 2*
[241] *Ch. 2*
[242] *Ch. 27*

immediate conversion...Sometimes I would find myself, in a great measure, *empty of this power*. I would go out and visit, and find that I made no saving impression. I would exhort and pray, with the same result. I would then set apart a day for private fasting and prayer, fearing that this power had departed from me, and would inquire anxiously after the reason of this apparent emptiness. After humbling myself, and crying out for help, the power would return upon me with all its freshness. *This has been the experience of my life.*[243]

Examples of the type of power that Finney experienced can be seen by looking at the effectiveness with which he witnessed to people the day after receiving his first two baptisms.

...I went down into the office, and there I was having the renewal of these mighty waves of love and salvation flowing over me, when Squire W— came into the office. I said a few words to him on the subject of his salvation. He looked at me with astonishment, but made no reply whatever, that I recollect. He dropped his head, and after standing a few minutes left the office. I thought no more of it then, but afterward found that the remark I made pierced him like a sword; and he did not recover from it till he was converted.

Soon after Mr. W— had left the office, Deacon B— came into the office and said to me, "Mr. Finney, do you recollect that my cause is to be tried at ten o'clock this morning? I suppose you are ready?" I had been retained to attend this suit as his attorney. I replied to him, "Deacon B-, I have a retainer from the Lord Jesus Christ

---

[243] *Power From On High, Ch. 2*

to plead his cause, and I cannot plead yours." He looked at me with astonishment, and said, "What do you mean?" I told him, in a few words, that I had enlisted in the cause of Christ; and then repeated that I had a retainer from the Lord Jesus Christ to plead his cause, and that he must go and get somebody else to attend his lawsuit; I could not do it. He dropped his head, and without making any reply, went out. A few moments later, in passing the window, I observed that Deacon B— was standing in the road, seemingly lost in deep meditation. He went away, as I afterward learned, and immediately settled his suit. He then betook himself to prayer, and soon got into a much higher religious state than he had ever been in before.

I soon sallied forth from the office to converse with those whom I should meet about their souls. I had the impression, which has never left my mind, that God wanted me to preach the Gospel, and that I must begin immediately. I somehow seemed to know it. If you ask me how I knew it, I cannot tell how I knew it, any more that I can tell how I knew that was the love of God and the baptism of the Holy Ghost which I had received. I did somehow know it with a certainty that was past all possibility of doubt. And so I seemed to know that the Lord commissioned me to preach the gospel...I sallied forth to converse with any with whom I might meet.

I first dropped in at the soul of a shoemaker, who was a pious man, and one of the most praying Christians, as I thought, in the church. I found him in conversation with a son of one of the elders of the church; and this young man was defending Universalism. Mr. W—, the shoemaker, turned to me and said, "Mr. Finney, what do you think of the argument of this young man;" and he then stated what he had been saying in defense of Universalism. The answer appeared to me so ready that in a moment I was enabled to blow his argument to the wind. The young man saw at once that his argument was gone; and he rose up without making any reply, and went suddenly out. But soon I observed, as I stood in the middle of the room, that the young man, instead of going along the street, had passed around the shop, had climbed over the fence, and was steering straight across the fields toward the woods. I thought no more of it until evening, when the young man came out, and appeared to be a bright convert, giving a relation of his experience. He went into the woods, and there, as he said, gave his heart to God.

I spoke with many persons that day, and I believe the Spirit of God made lasting impressions upon every one of them. I cannot remember one whom I spoke with, who was not soon after converted.[244]

In order to understand Finney's choice of the term "baptism" to describe his experiences one must understand a little about Presbyterian theology. Finney began his ministry as a Presbyterian and Presbyterians baptize by sprinkling or pouring. For Finney, the term *baptism* carried with it the idea of something being poured out and it was from this perspective that he understood what was happening to him. God, in essence, was pouring out His Spirit upon Finney.[245] After seeing Finney's understanding

---

[244] *Ch. 3*. Elsewhere Finney wrote describing the effects of his baptisms of the Holy Spirit that after receiving them "My words seemed to fasten like barbed arrows in the souls of men. They cut like a sword. They broke the heart like a hammer. Multitudes can attest to this. Oftentimes a word dropped, without my remembering it, would fasten conviction, and often result in almost immediate conversion. (*Power From On High, Ch. 2*)."

[245] The "pouring out of the Spirit" is a Biblical concept as the following Scriptures will attest:

of what he had experienced one is left to wonder if perhaps it would have been more Biblical if he had chosen to use the term "fillings of the Spirit" rather than "baptisms". In both the Old and New Testaments persons experienced temporary "fillings" of the Holy Spirit that empowered them to do extraordinary things that they normally could not do.[246] These were all temporary endowments that only lasted for a set period of time. This matches exactly with how Finney described his experience of finding that he was no longer endowed with the supernatural power of the Holy Spirit to minister effectively and had to seek new empowerments from the Holy Spirit.

"Until the Spirit is poured upon us from on high…" Is 32:15

"I will pour my Spirit upon your seed…" Is 44:3

"…for I have poured out my Spirit upon the house of Israel…" Eze 39:29

"…I will pour out my Spirit upon all flesh…" Joe 2:28

"…on my servants and on my handmaidens I will pour out in those days of my Spirit…" Ac 2:18

"…on the Gentiles also was poured out the gift of the Holy Ghost." Ac 10:45

[246] "…I have called by name Bezaleel…And I have filled him with the Spirit of God, in wisdom, and in understanding, and in knowledge, and in all manner of workmanship…" Ex 31:2-3

"…and Elisabeth was filled with the Holy Ghost: And she spoke out [prophetically] with a loud voice…" Lk 1:41-42

"And his father Zacharias was filled with the Holy Ghost, and prophesied, saying…" Lk 1:67

"And they were all filled with the Holy Ghost, and began to speak with other tongues, as the Spirit gave them utterance." Ac 2:4

"…and they were all filled with the Holy Ghost, and they spoke the word of God with boldness." Ac 4:31

"Then Saul…filled with the Holy Ghost, set his eyes on him. And said…behold, the hand of the Lord is upon you, and you will be blind, not seeing the sun for a season. And immediately there fell on him a mist and a darkness; and he went about seeking some to lead him by the hand." Ac 13:9-11

Finney came to understand that these baptisms, or fillings, were a source of power that was available to all believers:

> Christ expressly promised it to the whole Church, and to every individual whose duty it is to labor for the conversion of the world. He admonished the first disciples not to undertake the work until they had received this enduement of power from on high. Both the promise and the admonition apply equally to all Christians of every age and nation. No one has, at any time, any right to expect success, unless he first secures this enduement of power from on high.[247]

Finney understood that all Christians receive the Holy Spirit after converting but he realized that not all have the empowering of the Spirit for ministry present in their lives:

> Every Christian possesses a measure of the Spirit of Christ, enough of the Holy Spirit to lead us to true consecration and inspire us with the faith that is essential to our prevalence in prayer. Let us, then, not grieve or resist Him: but accept the [great] commission[248], fully consecrate ourselves, with all we have, to the saving of souls as our great and our only life-work. Let us get on to the altar with all we have and are, and lie there and persist in prayer till we receive the enduement.[249]

---

[247] *Power From On High, Ch. 1*
[248] Matthew 28:19-20
[249] *Power From On High, Ch. 4*

For Finney the way to receive this power was by following the example of the first disciples:

The example of the first disciples teaches us how to secure this enduement. They first consecrated[250] themselves to his work[251], and continued in prayer and supplication until the Holy Ghost fell upon them on the Day of Pentecost, and they received the promised enduement of power from on high. This, then, is the way to get it.[252]

There are many people in the church today who are claiming that they have received power from a baptism of the Holy Spirit. When asked how they received this baptism some say that they claimed it by faith and trust that they have it because there was a time when they believed God to give it to them. Others say that they know that they received it because of a supernatural experience that they had in which they were given an evidence of receiving it. However, in the overwhelming majority of these individuals that I have personally come into contact with there simply is little or no power for ministry. It doesn't matter what one claims by faith or what evidence one has if you don't have the power, *YOU DON'T HAVE THE POWER!* Too many Christians are resting on a past experience. In many of these cases these past experiences were not really the empowerment of the Spirit but just a misunderstood experience. These people were sincere, godly people and they truly thought that they had been endued with power from on high but their ministry results

---

[250] Set apart.
[251] Of reaching the lost.
[252] *Power From On High, Ch. 1*

show that this just was not the case. They are still fearful of what others will say or think of them for taking a stand, they try to witness but seem to have little or next to no effect upon their listeners, and their preaching just does not seem to make an impact.

Like Finney, all of us must seek new and fresh fillings of the Holy Spirit. It is not enough to rest in a one-time, past experience. This is shown very clearly in the example of Simon Peter. He was filled with the Spirit more than once and each time it gave him supernatural power for witnessing (Ac 2:4, 4:8). If a one time experience was not enough for Peter it certainly will not be enough for us. We must continually seek new and fresh empowerments of the Holy Spirit or else our ministries will shrivel up and die.

Chapter 11

Did Charles Finney Promote Emotionalism?

There is an unsettling trend amongst some contemporary ministers to justify the over-emotionalism of their services by appealing to well known ministers from the past whom they indicate operated their services in a like manner. Most people assume that a minister would not knowingly mislead them. However, when the original writings of the ministers who are appealed to are examined it is often discovered that they rejected over-emotionalism in their services.[253] In keeping with this trend it is probably only a matter of time before these appeals are made to the ministry of Charles Finney. Unsuspecting Christians, who believe in the ministries of these overly emotional ministers, will be swept away by these deceitful appeals to Finney so it is important to share a little of Finney's own writings in order to show how he viewed emotionalism in church services. Finney's life was spent witnessing revivals

---

[253] This is seen for example in appeals made to the ministry of John Wesley who, although appealed to by overly emotional ministers today, stressed to the early Methodists that they needed to be weary of emotionalism. See chapter 14 of *The Supernatural Occurrences Of John Wesley* entitled "John Wesley's Opinion On Miracles" for a fuller discussion of this. Peter Cartwright (1785-1872), a traveling Methodist evangelist, is another who is frequently referred to but anyone who reads his own feelings on this subject will realize that he rejected the over emotionalism of his day and would do the same in our time. See chapter 5 of *The Autobiography Of Peter Cartwright, The Backwoods Preacher* (London: Arthur Hall, Virtue & Co., 1862) for evidence of Cartwright's rejection of over emotionalism.

beginning in 1821. The following excerpt was written in 1845 and offers us a mature minister's insight into the right and wrong allowances of emotionalism in a church service.

Excerpts From "Unhealthy Revival Excitement"

Another error, which has prevailed to a considerable extent in promoting revivals of religion, I apprehend, is that of encouraging an <u>unhealthy degree of excitement</u>. Some degree of excitement is inevitable. The truths that must be seen and duly appreciated to induce the sinner to turn to God, will of necessity produce a considerable degree of excitement in his mind; but it should always be understood that <u>excitement, especially where it exists in a high degree, exposes the sinner to great delusions</u>. Religion consists in the heart's obedience to the law of the intelligence, as distinguished from its being influenced by emotion or fear. When the feelings are greatly excited, the will yields to them almost of necessity, I do not mean that it does absolutely by necessity, but that an excited state of feeling has so much power over the will that it almost certainly controls it. Now <u>the mind is never religious when it is actuated by the feelings, for this is following impulse</u>...

Now, just so much excitement is important in revivals as is requisite to secure the fixed and thorough attention of the mind to the truth, and no more. <u>When excitement goes beyond this, it is always dangerous</u>. When excitement is very great, so as really to carry the will, the subjects of this excitement invariably deceive themselves. They get the idea that they are religious in proportion as they are governed by their feelings. They are conscious of feeling deeply, and of acting accordingly, and because they do feel. They are conscious of being sincerely actuated by their feelings. This they regard as

114

true religion. Whereas, if they are really governed by their feelings as distinguished from their intelligence, they are not religious at all. This is no doubt the secret of so many false hopes, in those revivals in which there is very great excitement. <u>Where this has not been understood, and very great excitement has been rather nourished than controlled; where it has been taken for granted that the revival of religion is great in proportion to the amount of excitement, great evils have invariably resulted</u> to the cause of Christ. The great excitement attending revivals is an evil often incidental to real revivals of religion...I have often seen persons in so much excitement that the intelligence seemed to be almost stultified, and anything but reason seemed to have the control of the will. This is not religion, but enthusiasm; and oftentimes, as I shall have occasion to show in the course of these letters, has taken on, at last, the type of fanaticism...

There can be no doubt that when sinners are careless, addressing their hopes and fears is the readiest and perhaps the only way of arousing them, and getting their attention to the subject of salvation; but it should be forever remembered that when their attention is thus secured, they should, as far as possible, be kept from taking a selfish view of the subject. Those considerations should then be pressed on them that tend to draw them away from themselves, and constrain them to give their whole being up to God. We should present to their minds the character of God, His government, Christ, the Holy Spirit, the plan of salvation — any such thing that is calculated to charm the sinner away from his sins, and from pursuing his own interests, and that is calculated to excite him to exercise disinterested and universal love.

On the other hand, his own deformity, selfishness, self-will, pride, ambition, enmity, lusts, guilt, loathsomeness, hatefulness, spiritual death, dependence, its nature and its extent — all these things should be brought to bear in a burning focus on his mind. Right over against his own selfishness, enmity, self-will, and loathsome depravity, should be set the disinterestedness, the great love, the infinite compassion, the meekness, condescension, purity, holiness, truthfulness, and justice of the blessed God. These should be held before him, like a mirror, until they press on Him with such a mountain weight as to break his heart. It is very easy to see that this can not be done without producing a considerable degree, and oftentimes a high degree, of excitement. But it should be forever remembered that great excitement is only an incidental evil, and by no means a thing which is to be looked upon as highly favorable to his conversion. The more calm the soul can be kept while it gazes on those truths, the more free is the will left to comply with obligation as it lies revealed in the intelligence.

I have no doubt that much unreasonable opposition has been made to the excitement that is often witnessed in connection with revivals of religion; for, as I have said, great excitement is oftentimes unavoidable. But I have just as little doubt that, oftentimes, excitement has been unnecessarily great, and that real pains have been taken to promote deep and overwhelming excitement. I have sometimes witnessed efforts that were manifestly intended to create as much excitement as possible, and not infrequently have measures been used which seemed to have no tendency to instruct or to subdue the will, or to bring sinners to the point of intelligently closing in with the terms of salvation; but, on the contrary, it has seemed to me to beget a sort of infatuation through the power of overwhelming excitement. I can not believe that this is healthful or at all safe in revivals. Indeed, where such a course has been taken, I believe it will be found to be a universal truth that evil, instead of good, has resulted from such efforts. The more I have seen of revivals, the more I am impressed with the importance of keeping excitement down as far as is consistent with a full exhibition of truth...

Excitement can not reasonably be objected to as a thing entirely unnecessary in revivals; but the thing I would be distinctly understood to say is, that no effort should be made to produce excitement beyond what a lucid and powerful exposition of truth will produce. All the measures used to awaken interest, and our whole policy in regulating this awakened interest, should be such as will not disturb the operations of the intelligence, or divert its attention from the truth to which the heart is bound to submit.

I remark again, that many excitements which are taken for revivals of religion, after all, result in very little substantial piety, simply because the excitement is too great. Appeals are made too much to the feelings. Hope and fear are exclusively addressed. A strain of preaching is adopted which appeals rather to the sympathies and the feelings than to the intelligence. A tornado of excitement results, but no intelligent action of the heart. The will is swept along by a tempest of feeling. The intelligence is rather, for the time, being stultified and confounded than possessed with clear views of truth. Now this certainly can never result in good.[254]

An analysis of a few of Finney's revival services will show even more plainly that he took steps to curb emotionalism.

---

[254] *Revival Fire, Letter 2: Unhealthy Revival Excitement.* This letter originally appeared in *The Oberlin Evangelist*, April 23, 1845 mistakenly referred to as *Letter 6* in that issue. It should have been labeled *Letter 7*.

When preaching in London in 1849 the following scene occurred:

> As I was about to ask them to kneel down, and commit themselves entirely and forever to Christ, a man cried out in the midst of the congregation, in the greatest distress of mind, that he had sinned away his day of grace. I saw that there was danger of an uproar, and I <u>hushed it down as best I could</u>, and called on the people to kneel down; but to <u>keep so quiet</u>, if possible, that they could hear every word of the prayer that I was about to offer. They did, by a manifest effort, keep so still as to hear what was said, although there was a great sobbing and weeping in every part of the house. <u>I then dismissed the meeting</u>.[255]

When preaching in Rome, New York, Finney ended a meeting when he saw that the emotional excitement was getting out of hand:

> The meeting was called at the house of one of his deacons. When we arrived, we found the large sitting room crowded to its utmost capacity...We spent a little while in attempting to converse with them; and I soon saw that the feeling was so deep, that there was danger of an outburst of feeling, that would be almost uncontrollable. I therefore said to Mr. Gillett, "It will not do to continue the meeting in this shape. I will make some remarks, such as they need, and then dismiss them."...Mr. Gillett became very much agitated. He turned pale; and with a good deal of excitement he said, "What shall we

---

[255] *Ch. 29*

do? What shall we do?" I put my hand on his shoulder, and in a whisper said, "Keep quiet, keep quiet, brother Gillett."...Mr. Gillett became so agitated that I stepped up to him, and taking him by the arm I said, "Let us pray." We knelt down in the middle of the room where we had been standing. I led in prayer, in a low, unimpassioned voice; but interceded with the Savior to interpose his blood, then and there, and to lead all these sinners to accept the salvation which he proffered, and to believe to the saving of their souls. The agitation deepened every moment; and as I could hear their sobs, and sighs, I closed my prayer and rose suddenly from my knees. They all arose, and I said, "Now please go home without speaking a word to each other. <u>Try to keep silent, and do not break out into any boisterous manifestation of feeling</u>; but go without saying a word, to your rooms."

At this moment a young man...so nearly fainted, that he fell upon some young men that stood near him; and they all of them partially swooned away, and fell together. This had well-nigh produced a loud shrieking; but I <u>hushed them down</u>, and said to the young men, "Please set that door wide open, and go out, and let all <u>retire in silence</u>." They...went out sobbing and sighing, and their sobs and sighs could be heard till they got out into the street.[256]

When preaching in Bolton, England, Finney encouraged the Methodist brethren who were taking part in his revival meeting to tone down their emotionalism:

---

[256] *Ch. 13*

The Methodist brethren were very much engaged, and for some time were quite noisy and demonstrative in their prayers, when sinners came forward. For some time I said nothing about this, lest I should throw them off and lead them to grieve the Spirit. I saw that their impression was, that the greater the excitement, the more rapidly would the work go forward. They therefore would pound the benches, pray exceedingly loud, and sometimes more than one at a time. I was aware that this distracted the inquirers, and prevented their becoming truly converted; and although the number of inquirers was great and constantly increasing, yet conversions did not multiply as fast as I had been in the habit of seeing them, even where the number of inquirers was much less.

After letting things pass on so for two or three weeks, until the Methodist brethren had become acquainted with me, and I with them, one evening upon calling the inquirers forward, I suggested that we should take a different course. I told them that I thought the inquirers needed more opportunity to think than they had when there was so much noise; that they needed instruction, and needed to be led by one voice in prayer, and that there should not be any confusion, or anything bordering on it, if we expected them to listen and become intelligently converted. I asked them if they would not try for a short time to follow my advice in that respect, and see what the result would be. They did so; and at first I could see that they were a little in bondage when they attempted to pray, and a little discouraged, because it so crossed their ideas of what constituted powerful meetings. However they soon seemed to recover from this, because I think they were convinced that although there was less apparent excitement in our prayer meetings, yet there were many more converted from evening to evening.[257]

Compare also the following remarks from Finney on an overly emotional service that he attended at which the organizers used over-emotionalism to cause people to be "slain in the Spirit".

I attended a camp meeting in the State of New York which had been in progress two or three days before my arrival. I heard the preachers and attended the exercises through most of that day, and there appeared to be very little — indeed no visible — excitement. After several sermons had been preached, and after much exhortation, prayer, and singing, I observed several of the leading men to be whispering to each other for some time, as if in profound deliberation; after which, one of them, a man of athletic frame and stentorian voice, came down from the stand, and pressed his way along into the midst of a company of women who were sitting in front of the stand, and then began to clap his hands, and halloo at the top of his voice: "Power! Power! Power!" Soon another, and another, set in, till there was a general shouting and clapping of hands, followed presently by the shrieking of women, and resulting, after a little time, in the falling of several of them from their seats. Then it was proclaimed that the power of God was revealed from Heaven. After pushing this excitement to a

---

[257] *Ch. 35*

most extraordinary extent, the minister who began it, and those who united with him and had thus succeeded, as they supposed, in bringing down the power of God upon the congregation, retired from the scene of confusion, manifestly much gratified at the result.[258]

This scene, and some others of a similar character, have often occurred to my mind...In the getting up of this excitement there was not a word of truth communicated; there was no prayer or exhortation, — nothing but a most vociferous shouting of "Power! Power! Power!" accompanied by an almost deafening clapping of hands. I believe this to have been an extraordinary case, and that probably but few cases occur which are so highly objectionable. But things often occur in revivals which seem to beget an excitement but little more intelligent than this. Such appeals are made to the imagination and to certain departments of the sensibility as completely to throw the action of the intellect into the shade. So far as such efforts to promote revivals are made, they are undoubtedly highly disastrous, and should be entirely discouraged.[259]

Finney *did not* and *would not* support the overly emotional services that are sometimes witnessed in modern churches and often broadcast on television. Finney knew

---

[258] This sounds like many modern day overly emotional services in which the "power of suggestion" is used to make people think and feel that the Spirit of God is moving mightily in the meeting.

[259] *Revival Fire, Letter 6: Excitement In Revivals*. This letter originally appeared in *The Oberlin Evangelist*, May 7, 1845 referred to as *Letter 8* in that issue.

that getting a person excited was not salvation and could actually deter a man from getting saved. Ministers must stop inciting over-excitement and start emphasizing repentance if they will see souls saved as Finney did. Real preaching of the truth in sermons that search deep into the hearts of the congregation will produce emotion that leads to repentance.[260] Preaching in such a way as to encourage excitement will lead to people concluding that *emotion* is salvation and this will lead them to a wasted life of seeking one emotional experience after another until they die and realize that they worshipped *emotion* instead of God.

---

[260] 2Corinthians 7:10

Chapter 12

Why Was Finney So Successful As An Evangelist?

Modern readers are probably wondering *"Why was Finney so successful as an evangelist? There are evangelists today but their results are nowhere near Finney's."* An analysis of Finney's methods indicates that modern evangelists are not following the methods that Finney followed and this seems to be the reason for the difference in results.

Modern Evangelists Do Not Always Rely Upon Prayer To Make Their Ministry Efforts Prosper

Finney was a man who relied on prayer in order to have a successful revival.

> In regard to my own experience, I will say that unless I had the spirit of prayer I could do nothing. If even for a day or an hour I lost the spirit of grace and supplication, I found myself unable to preach with power and efficiency, or to win souls by personal conversation. In this respect my experience was what it has always been.[261]

And he warned those who thought that merely presenting the gospel *without* praying for success was enough that they were deceived:

---

[261] *Ch. 11*

Prayer is an essential link in the chain of causes that lead to a revival, as much so as truth is. Some have zealously used truth to convert men, and laid very little stress on prayer. They have preached, and talked, and distributed tracts with great zeal, and then wondered that they had so little success. And the reason was, that they forgot to use the other branch of the means, effectual prayer. They overlooked the fact that truth, by itself, will never produce the effect, without the Spirit of God, and that the Spirit is given in answer to prayer.

Sometimes it happens that those who are the most engaged in employing truth are not the most engaged in prayer. This is always unhappy.--For unless they, or somebody else, have the spirit of prayer, the truth by itself will do nothing but harden men in impenitence. Probably in the day of judgment it will be found that nothing is ever done by the truth, used ever so zealously, unless there is a spirit of prayer somewhere in connection with the presentation of truth.[262]

His experience with prayer began even before he was a Christian when he began attending a local prayer meeting and noted the failed prayer lives of the people who

---

[262] *Lectures On Revivals Of Religion* 2nd edition (New York: Leavitt, Lord & Co., 1835), Lecture 4: Prevailing Prayer, p.45-46. In connection with this Finney felt it also important to note that "Others err on the other side. Not that they lay too much stress on prayer. But they overlook the fact that prayer might be offered for ever, by itself, and nothing would be done. Because sinners are not converted by direct contact of the Holy Ghost, but by the truth, employed as a means. To expect the conversion of sinners by prayer alone, without the employment of truth, is to tempt God. (*Ibid*)"

attended. Upon studying his Bible and reflecting upon this event God revealed to him the method of successful prayer.

> But on farther reading of my Bible, it struck me that the reason why their prayers were not answered, was because they did not comply with the revealed conditions upon which God had promised to answer prayer; that they did not pray in faith, in the sense of expecting God to give them the things that they asked for.[263]

With this new understanding Finney became a man of prayer spending much of his time in secret prayer to God.[264]

---

[263] *Ch. 1*

[264] Early in his ministry Finney related that "I used to spend much of my time, when not abroad visiting, or engaged in preaching, in secret prayer to God. (*Ch. 12*)" While ministering in Boston Finney noted that "...so deeply was my mind exercised, and so absorbed in prayer, that I frequently continued from the time I arose, at four o'clock, till the gong called to breakfast, at eight o'clock. (*Ch. 27*)"

At one point Finney stated that "I found myself so much exercised, and so borne down with the weight of immortal souls, that I was constrained to pray without ceasing. Some of my experiences, indeed, alarmed me. A spirit of importunity sometimes came upon me so that I would say to God that he had made a promise to answer prayer, and I could not, and would not, be denied. I felt so certain that he would hear me, and that faithfulness to his promises, and to himself, rendered it impossible that he should not hear and answer, that frequently I found myself saying to him, "I hope thou dost not think that I can be denied. I come with thy faithful promises in my hand, and I cannot be denied." I cannot tell how absurd unbelief looked to me, and how certain it was, in my mind, that God would answer prayer — those prayers that, from day to day, and from hour to hour, I found myself offering in such agony and faith. (*Ch. 11*)"

The following story will demonstrate the kind of emphasis that Finney placed upon prayer in his revival meetings:

I have said, more than once, that the spirit of prayer that prevailed in those revivals was a very marked feature of them. It was common for young converts to be greatly exercised in prayer; and in some instances, so much so, that they were constrained to pray whole nights, and until their bodily strength was quite exhausted, for the conversion of souls around them. There was a great pressure of the Holy Spirit upon the minds of Christians; and they seemed to bear about with them the burden of immortal souls. They manifested the greatest solemnity of mind, and the greatest watchfulness in all their words and actions. It was very common to find Christians, whenever they met in any place, instead of engaging in conversation, to fall on their knees in prayer.

Not only were prayer meetings greatly multiplied and fully attended, not only was there great solemnity in those meetings; but there was a mighty spirit of secret prayer. Christians prayed a great deal, many of them spending many hours in private prayer. It was also the case that two, or more, would take the promise: "If two of you shall agree on earth as touching anything that they shall ask, it shall be done for them of my Father which is in heaven,"[265] and make some particular person a subject of prayer; and it was wonderful to what an extent they prevailed. Answers to prayer were so manifestly multiplied on every side, that no one could escape

---

[265] Matthew 18:19

127

the conviction that God was daily and hourly answering prayer.

If anything occurred that threatened to mar the work, if there was any appearance of any root of bitterness springing up, or any tendency to fanaticism or disorder, Christians would take the alarm, and give themselves to prayer that God would direct and control all things; and it was surprising to see, to what extent, and by what means, God would remove obstacles out of the way, in answer to prayer.[266]

Where are the praying evangelists and revival meetings today?

Modern Evangelists Do Not
Always Practice Or Believe In Fasting
To Make Their Ministry Efforts Prosper

Finney was a man who relied upon fasting in order to have a successful revival.

I used to spend a great deal of time in prayer; sometimes, I thought, literally praying "without ceasing."[267] I also found it very profitable, and felt very much inclined to hold frequent days of private fasting. On those days I would seek to be entirely alone with God, and would generally wander off into the woods, or get into the meeting house, or somewhere away entirely by myself.

Sometimes I would pursue a wrong course in fasting, and attempt to examine myself according to

---

[266] *Ch. 11*
[267] 1Thessalonians 5:17

the ideas of self-examination then entertained by my minister and the church. I would try to look into my own heart, in the sense of examining my feelings; and would turn my attention particularly to my motives, and the state of my mind. When I pursued this course, I found invariably that the day would close without any perceptible advance being made. Afterwards I saw clearly why this was so. Turning my attention, as I did, from the Lord Jesus Christ, and looking into myself, examining my motives and feelings, my feelings all subsided of course. But whenever I fasted, and let the Spirit take his own course with me, and gave myself up to let him lead and instruct me, I universally found it in the highest degree useful.[268]

For Finney, fasting was a means of attaining self-examination[269] and this is something that all ministers need to do in order to see if they are really being as effective for the Kingdom of God as they could be.

...when we want to look back and calmly examine the motives of our past conduct...it is often necessary to abstract our thoughts and keep out other things from our minds, to turn our minds back and look at things we have done, and the motives by which we were actuated. To do this effectually, it is often necessary to resort to retirement, and fasting, and prayer.[270]

---

[268] *Ch. 3*

[269] 2Corinthians 13:5

[270] *Lectures To Professing Christians Delivered In The City Of New York, In The Years 1836 And 1837,* (New York: John S. Taylor/Brick Church Chapel, 1837), Lecture 11: Bound To Know Your True Character, p.152

In his own ministry, Finney found that self-examination through prayer and fasting moved God to reveal to him areas that hindered his work for the Lord.

> Sometimes I would find myself, in a great measure, empty of this power. I would go out and visit, and find that I made no saving impression. I would exhort and pray, with the same result. I would then set apart a day for private fasting and prayer, fearing that this power had departed from me, and would inquire anxiously after the reason of this apparent emptiness. After humbling myself, and crying out for help, the power would return upon me with all its freshness.[271]

Fasting must become a regular part of any evangelist's life if they want to make an impact on society. In Mark 9:29 Jesus told his disciples that certain kinds of demons could only be cast out through prayer and fasting. If we are told that we cannot expect the devil to come out of a man unless we pray and fast why would we expect to cast Satan out of our communities through our preaching without it!

Modern Evangelists Do Not Always
Have The Church Handed Over To Them

When Finney would be invited to hold a revival he would be given complete control over the services. The minister of the church would, in essence, step back and allow Finney to hold and lead services in any direction that he felt led to. This included not setting a time limit for the

---

[271] *Power From On High, Ch. 2*

duration of the revival services. In some cases Finney was in control of the services for months at a time.[272]

This seems to match with the Biblical definition of an evangelist as demonstrated in the life and ministry of Timothy. Timothy was an evangelist[273] and was sent by Paul to initiate revivals (i.e. steer the church in the right direction).[274] The implication is that, by being sent by Paul, he would have had the same authority over the congregations that Paul would have had if he had personally went and everyone will agree that if Paul had went himself the church would have been handed over to him.

Secondly, in Ephesians 4:11 Paul lists five offices of church leadership stating that "...he gave some, apostles; and some, prophets; and some, evangelists; and some, pastors and teachers..." There are those who believe that this listing was written in an hierarchical order establishing that the office of the apostle was the highest level of leadership while that of teacher would be the lowest of the five. With that in mind, it is interesting to note that Paul listed the office of evangelist first and above the offices of pastor and teacher.

Modern Evangelists Do Not Always Preach To Incite A Revival Of The Members Of The Congregation

---

[272] This was because a real revival needs time to be cultivated and watered in order for it to bear fruit. A church does not decline over night and it will not, generally, be revived in one night either.

[273] 2Timothy 4:5

[274] Acts 19:21-22; 1Corinthians 4:14-17, 16:10-11; Philippians 2:19-23; 1Thessalonians 3:1-10

Many modern people have forgotten what the true definition of a revival is. The word itself is a composition of two words, *re* meaning to do again and *vive* meaning to live. In other words a *revival* is something which causes people to become alive again. This automatically implies that the people who are being preached to, in many cases, are dead spiritually and need to be *revived*. Most modern revivals that I have attended seem to take for granted that everyone in the church is spiritually alive and focus their preaching on seeing new people saved. Finney knew that it was pointless to expect new people to want to join a church if the church itself was spiritually dead. Hence, his sermons were designed in such a way as to convict the sinfulness of the church members knowing that their conviction and repentance would lead to new people being reached through them.

Preaching in order to incite conviction and repentance brought with it the necessity of being direct with people. In one example of this Finney had heard some people in the city cursing and later when they came to hear him preach he pointed them out and rebuked them in front of everyone for their language.[275] It seems that most

---

[275] "In passing around the village I heard a vast amount of profanity. I thought I had never heard so much in any place that I had ever visited. It seemed as if the men, in playing ball upon the green, and in every business place that I stepped into, were all cursing and swearing and damning each other…Sabbath morning I arose and left my lodgings in the hotel; and in order to get alone, where I could let out my voice as well as my heart, I went up into the woods at some distance from the village, and continued for a considerable time in prayer. However, I did not get relief, and went up a second time; but the load upon my mind increased, and I did not find relief. I went up a third time; and then the answer came. I found that it was time for meeting, and went immediately to the schoolhouse. I found it packed to its utmost capacity…I saw several of the men there from whom

modern day evangelists are too scared of offending people to preach like that and their results sorely fall below the results seen by Finney.

Modern Evangelists Do Not Always Have Personal Visitation With Each Of The Members Of The Church

Finney may have spent his evenings in the pulpit but a large percentage of his days were spent going house to house visiting the members of the church to discuss with them the issue of their personal salvation. Of all the revivals that I have attended I do not remember any evangelist ever coming to my house or the other members' houses to see if we were saved. Many modern evangelists are too intimidated to approach a church member and investigate with them to see if they are really saved. They find it easy to denounce "those sinners" outside of the church walls but what is really needed is to denounce the sinners inside of the church. And this needs to be done directly, one on one, in order to see a revival like Finney experienced.

I am convinced that in many cases churches just do not know what a revival is anymore as the following chart showing the differences will demonstrate.

A Finney Revival	A Modern Revival
1.) The effort is bathed in	1.) There is little or next to

I had, the day before, heard the most awful profanity. I pointed them out in the meeting, and told what they said — how they called on God to damn each other. Indeed, I let loose my whole heart upon them. I told them they seemed "to howl blasphemy about the streets like hell-hounds;" and it seemed to me that I had arrived "on the very verge of hell." Everybody knew that what I said was true, and they quailed under it (*Ch. 8*)."

133

prayer by the evangelist and by the church members.	no prayer. Perhaps the evangelist prays but the church does not.
2.) The evangelist regularly fasts and emphasizes to the congregation the importance of fasting.	**2.)** The evangelist may never fast. The church is not encouraged to fast by the evangelist because he does not think it is important.
3.) The evangelist is allowed to take over the church in order to steer it back in the right direction. The church realizes that the	**3.)** The evangelist is told what he can and cannot do. The duration of the revival is already planned out months in advance.

---

[276] Throughout Finney's *Memoirs* he made statements like the following regarding his methodology in conducting a revival:

"The means used were simply preaching, prayer and conference meetings, much private prayer, much personal conversation, and meetings for the instruction of earnest inquirers. These, and no other means, were used for the promotion of that work. (*Ch. 6*)"

"I have said before, that the means that I had all along used, thus far, in promoting revivals, were much prayer, secret and social, public preaching, personal conversation, and visitation from house to house; and when inquirers became multiplied, I appointed meetings for them, and invited those that were inquiring to meet for instruction, suited to their necessities. (*Ch. 13*)"

"The means that were used at Rome, were such as I had used before, and no others; preaching, public, social, and private prayer, exhortations, and personal conversation. (*Ch. 13*)"

"As it regards the means used in this revival, I would say, that the doctrines preached were those that I always preached, everywhere...The measures were simply preaching the gospel, and abundant prayer, in private, in social circles, and in public prayer meetings; much stress being always laid upon prayer as an essential means of promoting the revival. (*Ch. 26*)"

revival effort may take months to become effective.	
4.) The preaching is pointed and on target in order to incite conviction into all who are listening.	**4.)** The preaching focuses on "bigger sins" such as the ones affecting society outside of the church rather than on the sins within the particular congregation that have caused the church to need a revival.
5.) The evangelist spends a large portion of his days visiting house to house with the members to discuss their personal salvation with them. If he finds someone whom he does not think is saved he tells them directly and encourages them to repent so that they can be saved.	**5.)** The evangelist may visit the homes of a few of the leading people in the church but he does not attempt to visit all members to make sure that each one of them is saved. In some cases the evangelist is too timid to tell people face to face what he thinks about them.[276]

If I see a house that is built using red bricks and then try to recreate it using cedar wood will my house look like the red bricked one? Of course not and in the same manner we can never expect to see the results that Finney saw if we do not minister in the way that he did. His way may not be as easy as we have become accustomed to in our modern churches but why are we doing things the easy way when we can clearly see that our *revivals* do not *revive* our congregations?

Chapter 13

Conclusion

When I started this book, the second in the *Supernatural Occurrences Series*, my hope was to present evidence that would indicate how that God has always been willing to deal with individuals in the same manner that He did in the New Testament. I believe that I have done that. However, as I prepared this volume I soon realized that what we need now, more than anything else, is to focus on the church's need for revival. Our churches in Western Europe, Canada and the United States are filled with deadness and are sitting stagnant. Many of our churches (I hate to say it but I fear the majority of them) have abandoned prayer meetings, the importance of fasting, reaching out to the community to share the gospel, and accountability of their members. In their place they have promoted "fellowship" activities, said it was okay to enjoy worldly and immoral entertainment and focused more on gaining new *members* than they have in gaining new *disciples*.

Charles Finney is dead and he cannot come back to help us himself but we do have his methods and we are able to study him as a man who was used by God to revive church after church after church. Experiencing a revival in our congregations is not impossible. It is just that if we are ever going to see a real revival we are going to have to go back to the old methods. God is no respecter of persons[277] and if it worked for Finney it will work for us. We just have

---

[277] Acts 10:34

136

to make the effort. I will be the first to tell you that it can be scary to try and challenge the world and its way of doing things—*even scarier when the world is sitting in your congregation.* But if you won't do it, who will? Perhaps you are saying that you cannot because you have never received theological training. Finney never went to Bible College and he never went to seminary. He was a lawyer by profession yet God used his willingness to serve Him in a mighty way. You don't have to be a theologian to create a revival. All you need is a willing heart. Even if there is no evangelist *you* can pray, fast and start visiting with the members of your church to see if they are saved. Finney did not start by preaching from pulpits. He began by going out on the streets and witnessing to people and by volunteering to work with the youth in his church. *You* can make a difference and be the catalyst for revival in your church. Christian will you start a revival?

Made in the USA
Lexington, KY
06 May 2017